Russia and the World Trade Organization

Russia and the World Trade Organization

Peter Naray
Ambassador
Permanent Representative of Hungary to the United Nations
Geneva

© Peter Naray 2001

First published 2001 by
PALGRAVE
Houndmills, Basingstoke, Hampshire RG21 6XS and
175 Fifth Avenue, New York, N. Y. 10010
Companies and representatives throughout the world

PALGRAVE is the new global academic imprint of
St. Martin's Press LLC Scholarly and Reference Division and
Palgrave Publishers Ltd (formerly Macmillan Press Ltd).

ISBN 0–333–68218–1

This book is printed on paper suitable for recycling and
made from fully managed and sustained forest sources.

A catalogue record for this book is available
from the British Library.

Library of Congress Cataloging-in-Publication Data
Náray, Péter, 1942–
    Russia and the World Trade Organization / Peter Naray.
        p. cm.
    Includes bibliographical references (p.) and index.
    ISBN 0–333–68218–1 (cloth : alk. paper)
     1. Russia (Federation)—Commercial policy. 2. World Trade Organization–
    –Russia (Federation) 3. Soviet Union—Commercial policy. 4. Russia
    (Federation)—Economic policy—1991– 5. Russia (Federation)–
    –Economic conditions—1991– I. Title.
    HF1558.2 .N37 2000
    382'.3'0947—dc21
                                                      00–033290

10   9   8   7   6   5   4   3   2   1
10   09 08 07 06 05 04 03 02 01

Printed and bound in Great Britain by
Antony Rowe Ltd, Chippenham, Wiltshire

To my parents

Contents

Preface

The purpose of this book is to contribute to a better understanding of the problems that are faced by Russia in integrating itself into the world trade system as represented by the World Trade Organization (WTO). Such a complex issue can not be examined in isolation from the difficulties associated with Russia's transition from a centrally planned system to a market economy. Difficulties which are greatly responsible for the delay of Russia's accession to the WTO. The book, therefore, is not in a position to describe the history of the country's accession process because its end is not yet in sight. It tries, however, to give a brief analysis of the underlying problems.

During the writing of this book, the dramatic failure of Russian reform efforts confirmed the view that the approach taken to the country's transition process by many countries, international organizations and experts, and also by the Russian political leadership itself, was based on two major misconceptions. The first being that Russia was comparable to Central European transition countries and that the radical reform strategy applied in Poland or Czechoslovakia was, therefore, also applicable in the case of Russia. The second misconception was the idea that the success of the transition process depends mainly on appropriate economic policies and that the availability of supporting political, legal and economic institutions is a negligible concern. It was believed that the transition period would take at, maximum, a few years, but certainly not decades. The book attempts to identify where the roots of Russia's present difficulties lie and what their impact on the country's economic future, including its accession to the World Trade Organization, will be.

Obviously, it is not an easy task to explain why Russia has so many spectacular difficulties in transforming its command system into a smoothly functioning market economy. The question is frequently raised: what are the reasons that some countries, such as the Czech Republic, Hungary, Poland, Slovenia or even three former Soviet republics, the Baltic countries, have achieved remarkable success in the economic transition process, while many others have failed? The answer offered in this book (Chapters 3 and 4) is that the neo-liberal transition concepts, which have been applied in most countries, have completely neglected the differences in historical heritage between transition economies. They failed to recognize that modern market economies as they exist today in the western hemisphere are the products of centuries long gradual development. These societies not only follow market-oriented policies and strategies, but have a sophisticated network of political, legal, economic and social institutions which shape the whole social and business environment towards the interest of a proper functioning market economy. In some Central and Eastern European countries, which in terms of religion, culture and traditions have belonged to the west rather than to the east, this infrastructure was revived and developed. The book, however, does not want to suggest that the transition period in these countries was devoid of suffering, or that it has been finished everywhere with equal success. But it is a fact that these economies have 'turned the corner' and have entered a period of economic growth.

In Russia, however, the option of reactivating old institutions was non-existent, not only as a result of the three generations long Soviet socialism, but also because of the historical weakness of legal and market economy traditions during its earlier history, for example the absence of Roman law backgrounds, Russia's allegiance with the eastern Orthodox church, its turbulent history in the middle ages, and its pervasive heritage of autocracy. The introduction of liberal reforms in a country without appropriate institutions has lead to perverse consequences. Some examples are that while industry has been privatized, the new owners do not behave like real owners; and corruption and criminality are all pervasive – the criminal world is openly challenging the state. The example of Russia demonstrates that no economic reforms can be implemented with any hope of success, without a state based on the rule of law.

A more general lesson from this analysis is that Western Europe and societies which have been based on Western European traditions (for example North America, Australia and New Zealand) have maintained their 'institutional advantage' until present. For other continents, capitalism was an alien structure with institutional requirements which were difficult to meet. Crises in Russia, Asia and Latin America, and the problems of underdevelopment in Africa and elsewhere, have some common roots which can be related substantially to 'institutional and economic behavioural deficiency' due to different historical heritages. (It is not difficult to recognize that the failure of the WTO Ministerial Conference in Seattle in December 1999 was also due, to a large extent, to differences in the institutional heritage in developed and developing countries.) This deficiency manifests itself in the everyday practices of institutions in ways which do not correspond fully to the requirements of efficiency, at least, as measured in terms of a modern market economy. The big question is how that disadvantage can be redressed? Can historical heritages and engraved behavioural patterns be corrected through artificial interventions, let alone historical reprogramming? The question is particularly relevant in the age of globalization when pressure is growing to create institutions compatible with global requirements. The author suggests that for Russia, if it wishes to integrate itself into the world economy on its own value, the only choice is to undertake this reorientation at all levels, however painful and long this road may be.

The study gives a short critical overview of the ups and downs of Russian reforms and comes to the conclusion that the neo-liberal attempt to transform Russia overnight into a liberal market economy was doomed to failure. These utopian policies, which were introduced 'from above', without popular support – in a way reminiscent of Bolshevik methods – have largely contributed to the existing political and economic chaos, and the emergence of such informal structures as the mafia and mass corruption, which represent a growing threat not only to Russia but also to the rest of the world. On 17 August 1998, the Russian economy collapsed. There are no quick solutions to the problems. But the only proposals which have a chance of success are those which combine appropriate policies with the building of supporting democratic, legal and economic institutions in the framework of a modern state.

Chapter 1 includes an analysis on the accession of formal socialist countries to the General Agreement on Tariffs and Trade (GATT). The conclusion of the author is that during the cold war period accession criteria were very different from the present ones due to political considerations. Poland, Romania and Hungary were allowed to join the GATT despite the fact that their centrally planned trade regimes, especially those of Poland and Romania, were inconsistent with the letter and spirit of the GATT. Contracting parties of the GATT were ready to make derogation from the general rules in favour of some socialist countries simply to promote the politics of differentiation among Eastern bloc countries. The price paid by centrally planned economies for GATT participation was high; they became only 'second class' citizens in the club. With the collapse of the socialist camp, similar political considerations do not exist any more. Accession to the WTO, the successor organization of the GATT, is possible mainly on economic considerations.

Chapter 2 presents the Soviet Union's and Russia's approaches to the international trading system. The rigid rejection of the GATT in the late 1940s was replaced by a more lenient approach in the period of *détente*. The last years of the Soviet Union were characterized by a growing interest towards the GATT. The acceptance of the Soviet Union as an observer was one of the fruits resulting from the end of the cold war. Russia started its accession negotiations with the WTO in early 1995. Chapter 5 gives an overview of the new business oriented criteria *vis-à-vis* acceding countries which have developed during the first years of the WTO, and the considerations behind Russia's position and that of influential WTO members are explained. Chapter 6 examines the major issues discussed during Russia's accession negotiations. These include the examination of Russia's general economic policies, the framework for making and enforcing policies, policies affecting imports and exports of goods, internal policies affecting trade in goods, agricultural commitments, the country's trade-related intellectual property regime, policies affecting trade in services and trade agreements. The point is made that Russia has reached 'paper compatibility' in respect of many elements of its trade regime. However, there are very serious problems in the field of implementation of laws and regulations. Other kinds of difficulties, such as the degree of liberalization in trade in goods and services, are rooted in the lack of appropriate economic policy concepts.

Chapter 7 offers some conclusions on the state of Russia's accession negotiations. The author warns of 'accession fundamentalism' or the use of double standards which can be identified in some new accession protocols, and suggests following a pragmatic approach without allowing for systemic deviations from the spirit and letter of the WTO system. The practice of the WTO seems to indicate that in accession matters the era of major political considerations came to an end with the collapse of the Berlin wall. But it would be a fatal mistake to contribute to the political and economic isolation of Russia through badly chosen WTO accession conditions.

Acknowledgements

I wrote this book between early 1998 and September 1999. During that time I was Hungary's Ambassador and Permanent Representative to the United Nations and other international organizations in Geneva, a post to which I was appointed in September 1995. I benefited greatly from the thought-provoking world of Geneva based international organizations, which had very good experts in questions related to economic transition. I am particularly grateful to many diplomats, including members of the WTO Russian Accession Working Party, and experts of the WTO Secretariat and other international organizations with whom I had stimulating and regular exchanges of views in the subject of Russia's economic reforms, its integration into the world economy and accession to the World Trade Organization. I would especially like to thank Zdenek Drabek, Åke Linden, Constantine Michalopoulos, Ivan Anasstasov, Victor Ognivtsev, Paul Rayment and several members of the WTO Accession Division with whom I had the privilege of enjoying in depth discussions in the subject several times. I also wish to mention that the Russian programmes at the annual meetings of the World Economic Forum in Davos were extremely useful as they provided the opportunity to have direct contact with Russian leaders. I also benefited from the two special seminars organized by the Economic Commission for Europe in 1998 (which took place under my chairmanship) and 1999, which gathered many outstanding experts to discuss several aspects of economic transition and the financial crisis in Russia. I owe special thanks to Laurence Davey for his very useful comments of an editorial and linguistic nature, which have improved greatly the quality of my manuscript.

I wish to emphasize that the views expressed in this book are those of the author and should not be attributed in any manner to the Hungarian Government, my other former employers, or the people or organizations acknowledged above.

List of Abbreviations

AMS	Aggregate Measurement of Support
BISD	Basic Instruments and Selected Documents
CBR	Central Bank of Russia
CIS	Commonwealth of Independent States
CMEA	Council for Mutual Economic Assistance
EBRD	European Bank for Reconstruction and Development
ECE	United Nations Economic Commission for Europe
EU	European Union
GATS	General Agreement on Trade in Services
GATT 1994	General Agreement on Tariffs and Trade 1994
GKO	Treasury bill
IMF	International Monetary Fund
ITC	International Trade Centre, UNCTAD/WTO
m.f.n.	most-favoured-nation
MinFin	Hard currency denominated bond
OECD	Organization for Economic Co-operation and Development
OFZ	Federal loan bond
SPM	Sanitary and Phytosanitary Measures
TBT	Technical Barriers to Trade
TRIMs	Trade-Related Investment Measures
TRIPS	Trade-Related Aspects of Intellectual Property Rights
UNCTAD	United Nations Conference on Trade and Development
UNU	United Nations University
WIDER	World Institute for Development Economic Research
WTO	World Trade Organization

1
Accession of Non-Market Economies to the General Agreement on Tariffs and Trade

The GATT came into existence as a trade policy instrument for econo-mies where trade decisions were made on the basis of business con-siderations. The original contracting parties were all market economies. The Soviet Union, the only major non-market economy at that time, chose neither to be a signatory of the Charter of the International Trade Organization (ITO) nor the GATT. The United States, during the drafting stage of the ITO, acting in a spirit of compromise and tolerance towards the centralized Soviet eco-nomic system, made some attempts to bridge the gap between the centrally planned nature of the Soviet Union, its wartime ally, and the market-oriented spirit of the future international economic order. The Suggested Charter for an International Trade Organization of the United Nations, prepared by the United States, included the follow-ing provision for dealing with countries with complete foreign trade monopolies:

> Any member establishing or maintaining a complete or substan-tially complete monopoly of its import trade shall promote the expansion of its foreign trade with the other members in conso-nance with the purposes of the Charter. To this end such member shall negotiate with the other members an arrangement under which, in conjunction with the granting of tariff concessions by such other members, and in consideration of the other benefits of this Chapter, it shall undertake to import in the aggregate over a

period products of the other members valued at not less than an
amount to be agreed upon. This purchase arrangement shall be
subject to periodic adjustment.[1]

The Soviet Union, however, despite the fact that it adhered to the
Atlantic Charter and closely co-operated with its Western allies in
economic questions during the wartime period, did not support the
US proposal and, after brief hesitation, did not accept any role in the
creation of an international trade organization. The Soviet refusal to
participate in the negotiations was indicative of the mounting political tensions between the Soviet Union and the West as a whole. The
Soviet Union realized that its integration into the new international
trade system which was to be dominated by the major capitalist
countries would be a threat to its centrally planned economy and a
contradiction of its plans to dominate countries in Central and Eastern Europe. In view of the Soviet behaviour the US proposal was
withdrawn without any discussion on the merits.[2]

After its completion, the Soviet Union took a hostile attitude towards
the GATT.[3] Soviet policymakers considered it an instrument of US
economic expansion and dominance which pursued discriminatory
practices against the socialist countries. The pressure which the Soviet
Union exerted on Central and Eastern European socialist countries for
the early establishment of the Council for Mutual Economic Assistance
(CMEA) in 1949 can be understood as a Soviet reply to the creation of
the market based GATT system. The guiding principle for the CMEA,
(Comecon as it was called in the West), was the co-ordination of
national planing and the total disregard of market forces in the regulation of trade among its members. In 1955, when political relations
between East and West improved, the Soviet Union appealed in the
ECOSOC for ratification of the Havana Charter and creation of the ITO:
a position which reflected the Soviet Union's preference for comprehensive economic organizations which were more susceptible to political pressure, than for organizations dealing solely with trade. The
GATT was considered by the Soviets as a specific trade organization in
which they would not have enough bargaining power, at least not to the
extent they could have in political organizations. Later, the strongly
critical Soviet approach toward the GATT was gradually relaxed and in
the early 1980s the Soviet Union made its first steps towards regulariz-
ing its relationship with this Geneva based institution.

In sharp contrast to the hostile Soviet attitude, the socialist countries in Central and Eastern Europe, even in the darkest years of the cold war, showed a strong interest in participating in the multilateral trade system which was based on principles of non-discrimination and promotion of freer trade. This can be explained, firstly, by their different trade interests resulting from their smaller size, insignificant trade power and their much larger dependence on foreign trade compared to the Soviet Union. And secondly, one should not forget that these countries were until the late 1940s, market economies with substantial trade relations with the West: unlike the Soviet Union, which was at the time of the GATT's creation already a 'well established' centrally planned economy almost completely isolated from the rest of the world with only a distant memory of international trade co-operation and its institutions.[4]

Czechoslovakia, Poland, Romania and Yugoslavia in the GATT

Czechosklovakia was a founding member of the GATT and it maintained its status even after its introduction of a strict centrally planned economy. This meant that the setting of conditions for Czechosklovakia's participation in the GATT did not come into question.[5] But Hungary, Poland, Romania and Yugoslavia were already centrally planned economies when they took their first steps towards the GATT in the 1950s, and consequently, how to integrate them into the market oriented GATT system, while respecting its basic principles of non-discrimination and reciprocity, posed genuine problems.[6] To bridge this chasm, the contracting parties made serious efforts and demonstrated remarkable flexibility. Poland and Romania, as developing countries, acceded to the GATT in 1967 and 1971, against the background of their Soviet-type economic systems. In both countries foreign trade was a state monopoly, and major export–import and other trade decisions, were embodied in foreign trade plans. Domestic economic units had no, or very limited, influence on these plans. Accordingly, the accession working party report noted: '...foreign trade of Poland was conducted mainly by State enterprises and [that] the Foreign Trade Plan rather than customs tariff was the effective instrument of Poland's commercial policy.'[7] The Romanian foreign trade system was similar, with no customs tariff, and the country's foreign trade was based on directives of the Foreign Trade Plans.[8]

As neither Poland nor Romania had economically meaningful customs tariffs, they were not in a position, as required by the principle of reciprocity, to pay the GATT entrance fee for the tariff concessions and other advantages related to their accession to the GATT in the traditional form, namely through granting tariff concessions to other contracting parties in a multilateral, m.f.n. based system. Only the tariff commitments of those countries whose tariffs were recognized by other contracting parties as effective instruments of trade control could be accepted. It was obvious that Poland and Romania did not qualify. Instead, based on precedents set by some Soviet trade agreements, and the concept set out in the draft US ITO Charter referred to above, a commitment was accepted from acceding countries on the quantitative increase of their imports from the contracting parties as an appropriate entrance fee.[9] Poland undertook 'to increase the total value of its imports from the territories of contracting parties by not less than 7 per cent per annum.'[10]

Romania's commitment was similar in nature, but it was drafted in a more general way in order to avoid some of the problems experienced with the implementation of the Polish undertaking. Romania committed itself to develop and diversify its trade with the GATT contracting parties and stated its firm intention to increase imports from them at a rate not smaller than the growth of total Romanian imports provided for in its five-year plans. The motivations behind this drafting was to implement a more workable formula than Poland's and avoid an eventual discrimination in favour of Comecon members at the detriment of contracting parties.[11]

In addition to quantitative import commitments, Poland and Romania, for reasons also related to the nature of their economy, had to accept some other specific provisions in their protocols of accession. Some European contracting parties, in order to avoid the alleged danger of market disruption, insisted on the right to maintain, at least for a certain time, discriminatory quantitative restrictions, not consistent with Article XIII of the General Agreement, on imports from Poland and Romania. For similar reasons, both protocols include a so-called 'selective safeguard' clause, which gave the right to take restrictive measures selectively in case of alleged market disruption.

A special path was followed by socialist Yugoslavia to obtain contracting party status, which also offers some interesting lessons.
When Yugoslavia applied for observer status in 1950, it was a centrally planned economy. In the following years the country started to
decentralize its economy. In 1959, it became an associated member of
the GATT, but as it was still considered a centrally planned economy,
the special treatment it was given expressed the reservations of the
contracting parties about the country's economic system. However,
as an associated member, Yugoslavia continued economic reforms,
introduced economically meaningful tariffs, abolished multiple
exchange rates and diversified its trade relations. Economic decisionmaking became substantially decentralized as a result of the group
ownership called 'associated labour' which was a major pillar of the
special Yugoslav socialism. In 1966, in recognition of Yugoslavia's
independent political line, and its genuine economic and social
reforms, it obtained full contracting party status under normal conditions.

The example of Hungary, an early transition economy

The terms of Hungary's accession to the GATT deserve special attention because they reflect the country's market-oriented economic
reforms introduced in 1968. Using current criteria, Hungary could
have already been called a transition economy from the end of the
1960s. Hungarian reformers, however, were aware of the limited
possibilities that followed from the political and ideological division
of Europe and could never, therefore, state openly that the objective
of their reforms was the transformation of central planning into a
market economy without adjectives. The suppression of the 1956
Hungarian Revolution and the Prague Spring in1968 by the Soviet
Union reminded Eastern European politicians that they still lived in a
world shaped by Yalta and that any attempt to introduce consistent
political or economic reforms which diverged from 'existing socialism's' central tenets, triggered armed Soviet intervention. Question-
ing the hegemony of the communist party, the primacy of State
ownership, the wisdom of central planning or participation in
Soviet-led political and economic alliances, was taboo.

As a result of the reforms introduced from 1968, Hungary was no
longer a classical centrally planned economy like Poland or Romania.

Obligatory plan directives were abolished; targets of national plans were mainly to be achieved by economic incentives. The foreign trade regime was also reformed with the objective of linking the domestic economy to foreign markets. As the Report of the GATT Working Party indicated '... the Hungarian trading system had to be examined in the light of the existing system of economic management in Hungary, of which the adoption on 1 January 1968 of a customs tariff was an integral part.'[12] Most internal prices were linked to external ones subject to foreign trade multipliers, tariffs, and a tax and subsidy system. State owned enterprises were declared as autonomous legal entities, independent of each other and the State. Business considerations were to guide their economic decisions, including export and import transactions.

Hungarian reforms, however, remained inconsistent. The cold war did not allow for Hungarian reformers to introduce private property or to loosen the very close political and economic relationship with the Soviet Union and other socialist countries. A major reform of the political system was totally out of the question. As a result of these inconsistencies, the development of Hungary's economy remained largely determined by annual and mediumterm State plans. The state and the party retained major power in economic decisionmaking, including the sphere of enterprise. State administration also had far reaching discretionary powers in matters of trade, and no legal remedies against the decisions made by these bodies was available. The legal framework for economic activities was loose, and bargaining over subsidies and exemptions from rules between large state-owned enterprises and the state and party apparatus was frequent. State-owned enterprises enjoyed monopolistic positions in both production and trade. Bankruptcy was practically unknown; state subsidies were widespread for many reasons, including the support of full employment. Privatization was ruled out for ideological reasons. Despite successive reforms of state-owned enterprises, the dependence of enterprise management on state and party bureaucracy did not change substantially. Wage regulation remained centralized and about 30 per cent of prices were fixed by the State. Investment decisions of enterprises were influenced through a mixture of economic and administrative measures. The government retained its credit and foreign exchange monopoly; the banking system remained centralized. Capital movements between economic units were limited and foreign investments prohibited or very restricted. Foreign trade remained a State monopoly, but it was loosened compared to the pre-reform period. All export and import transactions were subject to discretionary licensing; imports of consumer goods were subject to a global quota. The share of CMEA countries in Hungary's foreign trade was about 50 per cent. Because of the isolationist CMEA system, Hungary had to maintain a separate set of trade instruments for dealing with CMEA countries, based on plan co-ordination and a system of trade agreements.

Hungary's terms of accession to the GATT, reflecting the contradictory nature of the country's economic and trade regime, was a mixture of conditions for centrally planned and market economies. In the issue of entrance fee, the Hungarian protocol followed the solution used for market economies and Hungary, despite the reservations of the European Community, was allowed to pay by tariff concessions.[13] Hungary categorically rejected any kind of quantitative import commitments because it considered them incompatible with its trade system.[14] The Protocol also allowed Hungary to maintain its existing trade regulations with CMEA countries regarding products originating in, or destined for, them. In return, Hungary undertook 'that its trading regulations or any change in them ... shall not impair its commitment, discriminate against or otherwise operate to the detriment of contracting parties.'[15] The provisions of the Protocol of Accession regarding the CMEA were of great political importance for Hungary as domestic hardliners and Moscow were concerned that market-oriented economic reforms in general, and Hungary's participation in the GATT in particular, could work against the interests of its socialist trading partners. One of the main reasons why Hungary's accession to the GATT was not blocked by internal opponents of the economic reforms, or the Soviets, was that the Hungarian Protocol of Accession did not impose any obligation on Hungary to the detriment of the country's participation in the CMEA.[16]

The Hungarian protocol, like the Polish and the Romanian, also included provisions on quantitative restrictions maintained inconsistently with Article XIII of the GATT and a selective safeguard clause.[17] The stated reason behind these specific conditions was similar also in the case of Hungary: namely the concern that the centrally planned elements of the Hungarian economic system may disrupt the market through low-priced exports.

Special protocols of accession at work

Protocols of accession for Poland, Romania and Hungary all called for biannual review meetings of special GATT working parties on the implementation of their provisions. Polish and Romanian Working Party meetings were similar due to both countries having accepted quantitative import commitments. Consequently, those meetings concentrated on the fulfilment of that obligation and had no mandate to discuss the functioning of any specific elements of the trade regimes. Meetings of the Hungarian Working Party were different, however, reflecting the substantial differences in the protocols of accession regarding the entrance fee. As Hungary reciprocated the advantages it enjoyed as a contracting party in accordance with general rules, contracting parties focused on the factors which determined the quality of the treatment accorded by Hungary to them.

In the first ten years after its accession, Poland increased its imports from contracting parties far above the 7 per cent annual target.[18] However, in 1977 and the following years, due to continued social and economic crises in Poland, the country did not fulfil its import obligations. The Polish Working Party met for the last time in 1977, as further meetings of the Working Party were considered, by both Poland and the contracting parties, to be innapropriate.

The Romanian import commitment was regarded as more workable than the Polish one, but it was less specific and more difficult to measure. The first two reports of the Romanian Working Party noted that 'Romanian imports from contracting parties were increasing satisfactorily in a manner corresponding with the intentions of the Protocol of Accession.' Later reports, however, did not include similar conclusions due to lower Romanian imports and doubts about Romania's compliance with the terms of its Protocol of Accession.[19]

The Hungarian Working Party had seven meetings between 1975 and 1989. The controversial issues at the meetings included the operation of the Hungarian price, subsidy and import licensing system, counter-trade practices and the consumer goods quota maintained by Hungary. The EC repeatedly asked Hungary to publish the product list annexed to the country's trade agreements concluded with CMEA partners. Hungary objected to this request on the basis that the publication of the annexes referred to by the EC would contravene the requirement of protecting the business secrets of

Hungarian enterprises. On most issues the meetings of the Working Party remained inconclusive.

At all meetings of the three working parties one of the main issues was the debate on the removal of quantitative restrictions maintained inconsistently with Article XIII of the GATT. The three countries were dissatisfied with the low rate of elimination of these restrictions and did not accept the claim of the parties maintaining these measures that it was due to economic and employment problems they faced. During the discussions in the working parties it became clear that the maintenance of the discriminatory quantitative restrictions could not be substantiated on economic grounds. Imports from the three countries in product groups, which were subject to these measures, were insignificant or, as was pointed out, they did not take place at all. These restrictions were maintained on imports from all socialist countries, contracting parties of the GATT or not, reforming their economies in a substantial way (like Hungary) or not at all (Albania for example). It was obvious that the discriminative quantitative restrictions were maintained for political reasons. This was clearly confirmed by the fact that very soon after the collapse of the Berlin wall, by 1 January 1990, the EC eliminated all discriminatory quantitative restrictions applied against imports from Hungary and Poland. The same treatment was extended to Czechoslovakia and Bulgaria in the same year.

As mentioned before, the accession protocols of Poland, Hungary and Romania each included provision for bilateral consultations in cases of alleged market disruption with the ultimate right to apply safeguard measures selectively. Under the Romanian and Hungarian protocols this right was reciprocal, or in other words the safeguard action was available not only for the contracting parties but also for Romania and Hungary. Under the Polish protocol this right was not reciprocal; Poland could not take selective safeguard measures based on its accession protocol. During the Working Party meetings the issue of selective safeguard action was also discussed in the context of the discriminatory quantitative restrictions. Hungary, for example, accepted the special safeguard clause 'in anticipation of early elimination of quantitative restrictions maintained against imports from Hungary, inconsistent with Article XIII.'[20] History shows, however, that concerns about the disruptive effects of Eastern exports were largely exaggerated. Imports from these economies did not cause any major market disruption. The selective safeguard clause was almost never used. The only consultations which took place under the clause took place in 1976, when the EC consulted with Poland, Hungary, Romania and some other centrally planned economies, on small electric motors and filament lamps.[21]

Why were the special protocols of accession not workable?

Hindsight of nearly two decades reveals that the specific terms of accession were not appropriate tools with which to build a bridge between market and non-market economies. As a result, none of these countries became fully integrated into the GATT. The path of quantitative import commitments which was used for economies maintaining a classical type of centrally planned economy proved to be totally un-negotiable. Measuring the implementation of commitments was near to impossible. The formulas contained in the protocols, especially the Polish one, had many weaknesses. There were no provisions to account for inflation or fluctuations in exchange rates and the issue of discrimination between imports from contracting parties and CMEA members was left open. It was rightly noted that possibly the Polish commitment was an irrelevant factor and had no influence over Polish import decisions.[22] The main problem with the Romanian formula was that it included terms which were difficult to interpret .[23] In case of both countries, actual import flows and import commitments were unrelated to each other. Import capacities of centrally planned economies were determined by a number of factors, many of them falling outside the purview of the GATT.

The Hungarian Protocol of Accession did not work entirely either, mainly because of the 'neither plan nor market' nature of the Hungarian economy. Inconsistent reform measures and a great deal of central planning did not allow a transparent and efficient GATT conform functioning of the trade regime. For this reason and because of Hungary's massif trade relations with its CMEA partners based on plan co-ordination and the resulting presence of a dual system of trade instruments, there was a never ending dispute as to whether rights and obligations of the parties were in balance or not. Discussions in the three working parties were characterized by mutual mistrust. The mistrust of the centrally planned economies stemmed from the fact that some contracting parties, mainly for political reasons, maintained discriminatory trade measures against their insignificant exports.

The experience of market economies shows that the integration into the GATT takes place at two levels; at the level of governments and at the level of enterprises. If trade decisions of enterprises are not influenced by the conditions established by their governments in the framework of the GATT, it demonstrates the lack of a market economy environment. Certainly, this was the case with the Polish and the Romanian (and also with the Czechoslovak) GATT participation, where even with the best intention one could talk only about a 'one-sided', government level integration. For the enterprises of these countries the contracting party status did not mean anything; their export and import activities continued to be determined solely by plan targets. This asymmetry was partially eliminated in the case of Hungary where enterprises, the microeconomic sphere, played an active role in making trade decisions in accordance with the conditions established by the GATT.

In the 1960s and 1970s, as it has been indicated above, the flexibility and ingenuity of GATT contracting parties in integrating centrally planned economies into the market-based GATT system was remarkable. One wonders why all these efforts were made to integrate into a market-based trade institution countries with fundamentally different economic systems. The answer lies in the sophisticated political relations of the cold war decades which were characterized by a deep and, most politicians believed, long-lasting division of the world into the capitalist and socialist camps. Immediately after the Second World War this ideological opposition was softened by the moral commitments by the United States and other allied powers towards the Soviet Union, a key wartime ally in the victory over Hitler's Germany. Against this background it was understandable that the United States and other Western countries which played a role in shaping the world trade system in the postwar era tried to involve the Soviet Union in the negotiations on the ill-fated ITO. However, after a short period, ideological positions faded the memory of wartime co-operation and the Soviet Union withdraw from global economic negotiations. Soon, the world became divided into two major political and economic camps, and it remained so for decades.

But the socialist camp was never as monolithic as it seemed. Smaller Central and Eastern European countries soon realized that the CMEA and the so-called 'socialist division labour' did not satisfy their economic needs; they needed closer ties with the West. Several initiated official relations with the GATT. The West, influenced by its security considerations, increasingly started to follow, from the 1950s, a policy of differentiation. Those countries which differed in their internal or external policies from the Soviet Union, such as reformist Yugoslavia, a non-aligned socialist country, not a member neither in the Warsaw Pact nor in the CMEA, or Poland and Romania which followed a relatively independent foreign policy line, or Hungary with its economic reforms, received a more favourable treatment in the GATT than those countries of the Eastern bloc which remained close to the Soviets. As it was explained,

> The West now recognized that intensification of economic contacts with centrally-planned economies could be a positive development, provided that East–West trade policy was subordinated to the objectives of East–West foreign policy. According to this view, trade with the East was to become an instrument for the modification of Eastern Europe's centrally planned systems and a means of helping some of those countries to increase their relative independence within the Eastern bloc.[24]

The use of economic and trade policies for foreign policy purposes was characteristic of both the United States and Western Europe. Their approach, however, was different: Western Europe 'was more strongly influenced by trade interests: the United State by political'.[25]

This major shift in policy explains why Poland and Romania with old-fashioned centrally planned economies could become contracting parties and why Bulgaria that remained a close Soviet ally could not join even the GATT Standards Code. One has to add, however, that, beyond the contracting party status, in terms of specific trade advantages or market access, none of these countries received a better treatment than other socialist countries. Their acceptance in the GATT provided some systemic advantages and had a symbolic value.

It followed from the definition of the policy of differentiation that the Soviet Union was not eligible for GATT contracting party or observer status throughout the whole period. Difficulties over

China's WTO membership are also intertwined with political considerations. The specificity of the Hungarian case was that Hungary was different to the extent that it introduced major market oriented reforms, but there was little doubt in the eyes of the contracting parties that as a whole the Hungarian trade regime was still far from full GATT compatibility.[26] Therefore, one can safely state that the role of political considerations was so overwhelming that decisions of the Western contracting parties to integrate Poland, Romania and Hungary to the GATT were probably made well before the formal negotiations on accession started.[27]

Of course, for the accession of centrally planned economies to the GATT on specific terms, the trade system as a whole paid a price. Polish and Romanian quantitative import commitments, the selective safeguard clauses and the toleration of quantitative restrictions, which were inconsistent with the GATT, were serious deviations from the liberal market economy approach of the GATT. It should be noted that the issue of quantitative discriminatory restrictions especially divided market economy countries. The issue of quantitative import commitments was by far the most dangerous deviation from the letter and spirit of the General Agreement as it legalized the use of managed trade and administrative State intervention. The maintenance of the measures by the EC was heavily criticized by the United States, Canada, Japan, Switzerland and some other countries over fears of erosion of the rules and the system as a whole.[28] Obviously, the policy of differentiation overruled all GATT or other professional considerations. As a result of the accession of centrally planned economies which could not integrate fully into the GATT system, the notion of 'second class GATT citizenship' was informally developed with the connotation that non-fulfilment of GATT obligations *vis-à-vis* these countries was more tolerable than in respect of its first class citizens. Fortunately, the danger of a more institutionalized deviation from the rules of the GATT was recognized and the integration of Part V (Special rules for non-market economies) into the text of the GATT did not take place.[29]

The second class citizenship of these countries was *de facto* ended with the collapse of the socialist system, the dissolution of the Warsaw Pact and the CMEA, and the introduction of consistent market economy reforms from the beginning from 1989. In 1990/91, the reforming Central and Eastern European countries asked for changes in their protocols of accession with the objective of eliminating obsolete or inoperative provisions. The work had not been finished. The respective GATT Working Parties were, however, established but only the Polish Working Party had meetings, but did not complete the work.[30] On 1 January 1995, the WTO Agreement came into force with the original membership of all countries with special protocols of accession. Legally, the old specific terms of accession remain valid, as the protocols of accession have become part of GATT 1994. However, it is obvious that these specific terms should be considered obsolete.

Lessons from the GATT participation of Central and Eastern European countries for Russia and other transition economies wishing to join the WTO

The much admired flexibility of the GATT in developing devices to bridge the gap between its market based rules and centrally planned economies was the product of the cold war. Contracting parties accepted certain centrally planned economies in the GATT system for political reasons under the policy of differentiation. If a centrally planned country indicated some signs of independence from the Soviet Union, either in domestic or foreign policy, and there was some hope that the participation of that country in the GATT could contribute to the loosening of the enemy's cohesion, the request for accession was received favourably. In those cases, basic philosophical differences did not constitute insurmountable barriers, as the accession conditions of Poland and Romania demonstrated.

Since the sudden collapse of the socialist system and the Soviet Empire, political considerations in WTO accession matters have become less important and all requests for accession are decided mainly on the basis of economic considerations. As a result, the flexibility and tolerance of WTO members have become rather limited in the shaping of the protocols of accession. As we may observe, this is also true for Russia and other major transition economies. While in the 1980s, in the context of the Yalta world order, all experts suggested new interfaces for the integration of the Soviet Union and other planned economies which were still outside the GATT, now, the contrary is true; there is a great pressure on acceding countries to assume practically all WTO obligations fully and right from the beginning of membership for the sake of trade interests of individual members and the system as a whole alike.[31]

This does not mean, however, that the era of political considerations is over, therefore there is no place for flexibility or a gradual approach in accession matters. Currently, though, the direction and quality of political considerations is different. The world now has a genuine interest in integrating Russia into the WTO for the sake of trade and policy considerations alike. What was said previously '...that participation in the GATT and economic reform feed on each other' is even more valid for the WTO. The lessons gained from the accession of centrally planned economies to the GATT should not be totally forgotten.[32]

2
The Road Leading from Soviet Rejection of the GATT to Russia's WTO Accession Negotiations

From opposition to GATT, to application for observer status

As explained in the first chapter, the Soviet Union, after a short period of support, followed the preparatory work on the ITO and the GATT with increasing hostility. This approach was based mainly on political considerations: in these years the Soviet Union considered the world-wide socialist system as an alternative to capitalism. Hardliners, who professed the imminent collapse of the capitalist system and the victory of socialism rose to the ideological forefront. For this reason, the Soviet leaders, neglecting the country's obvious economic interests, decided against any real co-operation with the non-communist world and intensified their support of global socialist revolution. It was of no surprise that the Soviet Union took all possible opportunities to criticise the GATT which it considered an 'instrument of economic expansion into the world market for U.S. monopolies.'[33] This openly hostile approach was maintained for about 15 years. Reportedly, the last open criticism of the GATT by a leading Soviet official was made in 1960.[34]

Later, in the years of *détente*, the Soviet approach toward the GATT became much softer. One of the reasons was that in this period a number of CMEA countries joined the GATT. Their accession conditions indicated that, in the framework of GATT, differences between market economies and centrally planned socialist countries could be bridged. It was of decisive importance for the Soviets that they could see it was possible for socialist countries to participate in the multi-lateral trade system without either being obliged to give up the basic elements of a Soviet-type centrally planned economy, or being made to ignore the requirements of the Soviet concept of equality between states and non-discrimination in intergovernmental relations. This did not mean, however, that the Soviet Union herself was ready to seriously consider its own accession to the GATT. Soviet foreign trade policy was not prepared to replace its bilateral approach with a multi-lateral system in which the Soviet Union could not play a role corresponding to its weight in world politics. In addition, economic pressure on GATT accession on the energy and raw material exporter Soviet Union was much smaller than for smaller socialist countries, which exported much more manufactured goods. Probably, these were the main considerations behind the Soviet Union's decision not to accept the invitation to participate in the Tokyo Round of trade negotiations between 1973 and 1979 which was implied by the terms of the Tokyo Declaration.[35]

From the early1980s, against the background of a worsening domestic economic situation and a deteriorating international political profile due to their invasion of Afghanistan, the Soviet Union started actively investigating the possibility of joining the GATT. CMEA members which were already contracting parties were asked to share their experience with Soviet experts.[36] Most Western countries, however, did not take a friendly attitude towards this shift in Soviet policy. In 1982, when the Soviet Union wanted to participate at the November 1982 GATT ministerial meeting as an observer, it was discouraged by the United States and other Western contracting parties. An informal Soviet request for observer status in the GATT Council and some Tokyo Round Code Committees also met with strong resistance. In December 1982, in Geneva, a Soviet delegation informally approached several contracting parties and members of the GATT Secretariat with a view to exploring possibilities of the Soviet Union being granted observer status. At that time there was no consensus among contracting parties to allow this: the United States reaction to the Soviet request was negative because of their concern that the participation of the Soviet Union would poltitise the GATT and, *inter alia*, it could adversely effect other eastern European GATT contracting parties;[37] the European Economic Community was reported to be divided over the Soviet request. Several Western governments, including France, the Scandinavian countries, Canada and most developing countries reportedly felt that the Soviet Union should not be rebuffed.[38]

The next important Chapter in Soviet–GATT relations was opened in March 1986 when the Soviet Government expressed its recognition that the next round of multilateral trade negotiations would likely be 'universal and global' in its implications and declared that 'it is essential that the forthcoming round be of an open character and that all countries concerned should participate in the negotiations.'[39] On 15 August 1986, the Soviet Union submitted its request to the GATT Secretariat to 'participate' in the Uruguay Round trade negotiations.[40] The request stated that the Soviet Union sought to increase its foreign trade and aimed to strengthen trust and co-operation with GATT countries. It also included a statement that Soviet participation in GATT would help develop international trade by contributing to the improvement of trade policy conditions. The Soviet request was squarely rejected by major contracting parties[41]. In fact, conditions for participation were drafted in a way which allowed the participation of almost any country except the Soviet Union (and Bulgaria) and provided specifically that non-contracting parties to the GATT would have no say in any decisions which would change the GATT rules or make additions to them. In the context of this rejection, the United States Trade Representative also emphasized the Soviet international trading system's 'fundamental, practical and philosophical variance with the principles and practices of GATT'.[42]

The Western rebuff was based on political considerations. It would be difficult otherwise to explain why it was more acceptable for a pre-perestrojka orthodox Soviet empire to participate in the Tokyo Round in 1973 than for Gorbachev's Soviet Union to participate in the Uruguay Round of 1986. The Soviet request to participate in the Uruguay Round in itself, however, constituted a turning point in the country's approach to international economic organizations. Prior to this, all Soviet approaches regarding the GATT were informal. Evidently, under the influence of the policy of differentiation, a number of contracting parties thought that accession to GATT was only available to smaller Central and Eastern European countries – even if they maintained rigid central planning without the slightest hope of reforms, as the acceptance of Ceaucescu's Romania proved.

The basis of the different treatment accorded to the Soviet Union was that it imposed its ideology on the countries of Central and Eastern Europe and thereby prevented their political and economic development. Therefore, the exclusion of smaller Central and Eastern European countries from the GATT would have resulted in their double punishment; the first punishment being that the world let the Soviet Union extend its total influence on these countries after the war; the second one, the introduction of sanctions because of policies followed under Soviet pressure. In 1986, the West did not apparently subscribe to the notion that Soviet participation in the GATT could contribute to a further loosening of the traditional Soviet system or that it could give decisive support to reform-minded forces. From the systemic point of view, the rejection of the Soviet initiative was perfectly justified. The Soviet trade regime was incompatible with the GATT and fears were well-based that the participation of a major non-market economy in the GATT could have diluted or eroded the market-oriented rules.[43] Nevertheless, the rejection of the Soviet request was regretted by many observers.[44]

This regret, however, seemed to forget that the decision to reject the Soviet proposal was made in the context of a cold war philosophy in which the Soviet Union was treated by the Western countries differently than other non-market economies. But as soon as it became clear that a closer relationship with the GATT could be used by reform-minded Soviet leaders to help dismantle 'existing socialism', or in other words, that the end of the cold war was visible, the West's philosophy changed completely. During the Malta summit in December 1989, President Bush suggested granting an observer status to the Soviet Union in the GATT after the conclusion of the Uruguay Round.[45] The European Community also announced its support for Soviet observership. However, at that time, neither the United States nor the EC supported full membership.[46] Officially, the Soviet Union applied for observer status at sessions of the Contracting Parties and the Council in March 1990. According to the application, the objective of requesting observer status was 'to get acquainted with the methods of work of various GATT bodies and to be able to keep GATT Contracting Parties regularly informed of the process of restructuring the economy of the Soviet Union'.[47] Informal consultations on the Soviet request revealed that the United States and Japan had reservations while many other contracting parties, including the EC and its member states, were in favour of approving the application immediately. As it was reported, officials in the Office of the US Trade Representative (USTR) 'opposed granting observer status for fear that this would undermine the integrity of the international trade institution.' At the same time officials in the State Department working on bilateral relations with the Soviet Union preferred to grant observer status as a positive symbolic gesture to the USSR. In the context of Japan's reservations the unresolved territorial dispute over the Kurile Islands was mentioned, in addition to Japan's concerns regarding the incompatible nature of the Soviet economy with the GATT system.[48] By 16 May 1990, all opposition to the Soviet observer status was lifted and the GATT Council approved unanimously the Soviet request.

A large number of Council members welcomed this historic decision. The representative of the European Communities stressed that the decision 'brought further support to the universal vocation of the multilateral trading system.' The representative of the United States admitted that the inclination of the United States had been to defer a decision on the request 'until after the completion of the Uruguay Round, and until the course of economic and political change in that country had become clearer; but in recent weeks it had become obvious that nearly all other delegations had not shared this view; therefore, the United States had joined in the consensus at the present meeting.' He also stated, supported by the representative of Japan, that observership 'was clearly a totally separate matter' from accession and the decision in respect of observer status 'in no way prejudged any action on a possible future request for accession'. Many speakers expressed the belief that the observer status of the Soviet Union would promote the cause of market economy reforms and the creation of a GATT conform trade regime.[49] There was no doubt that the decision of the Council, by giving an official status to the Soviet Union in this unique multilateral trade institution, marked the end of the cold war in the GATT. It was a major step towards future accession negotiations with Russia, the successor to the Soviet Union.[50]

The start of Russia's negotiations for accession to the WTO

On 11 June 1993, in Moscow, after two years of Russian GATT observership, President Boris Yeltsin handed over a document to Director-General Arthur Dunkel containing the following communication:

The Government of the Russian Federation applies for accession of the Government of the Russian Federation to the General Agreement on Tariffs and Trade under its Article XXXIII and hereby requests that this application be given due consideration by the Contracting Parties in accordance with the usual procedures, including the establishment of a Working Party to examine the accession of the Government of the Russian Federation to the GATT.[51]

He was quoted to say, with a smile on his face, while handing over the Russian application to the Director-General: 'I hope that you will not put this on the back burner until the end of the decade. I hope that you will take a decision by the end of 1993.'[52] The application was put on the agenda of the next Council meeting on 16 June. In introducing the Russian application at the Council meeting, the Russian representative stated that the application was a logical constituent part of the Russian economic reform policy, that the accession of Russia to the GATT was considered by its government as an essential step towards the country's integration into the international trading system. Describing the results of Russian reform efforts, he pointed out that the country had become an internationally open economy based on market principles; that administrative regulations of imports had been removed and that customs tariffs had become a major instrument of import regulation; currency regulation had been liberalised and internal convertibility of the rouble had been established with a single market exchange rate. As a consequence of price liberalization and privatization, Russia appeared to be a liberal economy. He expressed Russia's commitment to a more open, viable and durable multilateral trading system based on GATT rules and principles. He also emphasized that Russia's accession would improve trading opportunities both for Russia and its trading partners.[53]

Members of the Council, including practically all Russia's major trading partners, warmly welcomed and supported Russia's application. By a number of delegations the Russian request was described as a major historical event. It was emphasized that Russia's accession would strengthen and further enhance the multilateral trading system and would assist Russia's integration into the world economy. The point was also made that the Russian reforms, which were described as courageous, would be supported and enhanced through the accession. It was stated that 'The transition from 70 years of a command economy was proving to be a huge and complex process.'[54] The Council, in accordance with the standard GATT procedure, established a Working Party on the Accession of the Russian Federation with the usual terms of reference.[55]

In April 1994, The Final Act of the Uruguay Round was signed; GATT accessions had to be transformed into WTO accession procedures. In December 1994, the Russian Government requested that the WTO Preparatory Committee initiate the process of accession of Russia as a developed country[56] to the WTO in pursuance of paragraph 2 of the Decision on Acceptance of and Accession to the Agreement Establishing the WTO and in accordance with Article XII of the WTO Agreement.[57] The Preparatory Committee gave a green light to the Russian request. Since the beginning of 1995, Russia has been negotiating for its accession to the World Trade Organization.

3
Recent Political, Economic and Institutional Developments in Russia

Why does history matter?

Integration of a country into the world trade system presupposes the fulfilment of two conditions. First, the existence of trade-related laws and regulations, which are compatible with the relevant international obligations, namely with the rules of the WTO. And second, the presence of economic units which shape business activities in accordance with the requirements established. Recent examples show that it is much easier to adopt WTO conform laws ('paper compatibility') than to have an economy whose participants actually act in total harmony with the expectations set by laws ('real compatibility'). The latter has probably never happened. Nevertheless, there are countries which are closer to that requirement than others. The big question is: why are the economic systems which exist today, all based on market economy principles, so different? Why do they differ so greatly in terms of economic, institutional and political development and business culture? Who could deny that today's capitalism of Western Europe or the United States differs substantially from that of India, Pakistan, Latin America or Africa? And of course, economic systems in Russia and in many other transition economies, reveal even more dissenting features. The answer is simple; different historical backgrounds. The differences between countries' business cultures, institutions or indeed, the behevior of their citizens and subjects, are as different as the unique histories which shaped those countries. This historical 'determinism' is relevant for defining a country's relationships with global organizations, or in this case, with the WTO; therefore it is worth a thorough examination.

It is interesting to note, however, that in the case of Russia this evident historical approach has been almost totally neglected by both Russian and foreign politicians and experts. But Russia's present day economic difficulties are rooted in its past. From the end of 1991 efforts have been made to transplant a liberal market economy into Russia, which has been the product of a centuries long development in the West. The hardships of current reforms can not be solely explained by seven decades of Soviet socialism. The roots of hostility to these reforms are much deeper. The special quality of the Russian political and business environment is a direct consequence of Russia's different historical path over hundreds of years. The divergence of Russian history from the rest of Europe, which is important from the point of view of politics, economics and institutional developments, was marked by the lack of Roman law traditions, the schism between the Byzantine and Roman churches, the absence of reformation, Russia's turbulent history in the Middle ages and the resulting slow development of capitalism, which was considered as an alien element by many. These circumstances were all responsible, that compared to the West, pre-1917 Russia, compared to the west, was an underdeveloped country with a very weak legal and institutional system. The autocratic Russian state intervened massively in economic processes at the end of the 19th century, and at the beginning of the 20th century, which were the decades of '*lassez faire*' capitalism in Western Europe and the United States. Weak Russian capitalism, autocracy, and the poverty and suffering of the Russian peoples, greatly increased by the First World War, prepared the way for the Bolshevik revolution. The gap between Russia and most of the rest of the world further widened during the Soviet period, the whole philosophy of which was based on the denial of market values. The Soviet system which thought it was a promising alternative to capitalism did all it could to destroy all traces of a capitalist system in Russia.

Recent events not only in Russia, but also in other parts of the world, (for example Asia and Latin America) have proved that for reforms to be successful, in the age of globalization, not only sound economic policies are needed but also adequately developed political, legal and economic infrastructures. In Russia, neither part of this equation has been present. The integration of Russia into the world economy, including its membership in the WTO, needs carefully worked out long-term policies for the development of relevant institutions and the whole business environment. In designing and implementing these policies, the ways in which history has conditioned or influenced the behaviour of economic units, and the population in general, must be taken into account. Of course, it is not easy to decipher historical traditions and explain how they manifest themselves in every-day thinking and the current behaviour of business participants, nor to determine exactly to what extent they have an impact on the functioning of legal and economic institutions. But the author is convinced that this historical approach is the only way to avoid the simplifications of the last few years, which occurred because history was disregarded.

The size of this study does not allow a detailed historical analysis of Russia's past. Nevertheless, a short description of Russia's recent economic reforms and some references to relevant historical developments are included in order to create a better understanding of the tasks which are facing Russia on its long road towards integrating itself fully in the international trade system.

Heritage from the Soviet epoch

The establishment of the Soviet political, legal and economic system was finished by the mid-1930s. All the institutions of the old regime were destroyed and a totalitarian dictatorship was imposed. The whole economy was nationalized and became centrally planned, millions of people who were suspected of the slightest opposition to the new system were murdered or sent to labour camps. The essential elements of this Stalinist political and economic regime remained without major changes until 1985 when Gorbachev came to power, at a time when the economy of the country was in serious trouble. Decades of central planning and almost total isolation of the country's economy from the outside world resulted in massive missallocation of resources and the creation of thousands of huge and inefficient industrial dinosaurs with large monopolistic powers. Soviet agriculture never recovered the from forced collectivization of the 1930s. The day-to-day survival of the country and the maintenance of its superpower status was made possible only by vast oil, gas and raw material exports which amounted to about 80 per cent of convertible currency exports. Gorbachev quickly realized that, after years of stagnation, reform of the economy was indispensable for the survival of a socialist regime.

Economic half reforms during the Gorbachev years

Looking back on the Gorbachev years, one can state fairly that economic reforms between 1985 and 1991, were not successful. Probably, the major difficulty was that Gorbachev 'had no blueprint for reforming a centrally planned economy'[58] and reforms, again, as so often in Russian history, were made from above, without massive support of the people. The lack of determination to replace the planned economy with a consistent market economy prevented Gorbachev and his entourage from introducing the necessary radical changes in the basic economic institutions of the country, such as ownership structure, central planning, foreign trade and pricing. The adopted laws and other measures either constituted pseudo reforms, as for example the campaign against alcoholism, or they constituted only half measures. The attitude towards private enterprise remained suspicious throughout the whole period.

Some examples: the Law on Co-operatives in May 1988 facilitated the creation of private business, but these undertakings proved to be too successful in the eyes of the authorities, so several restrictions were imposed on them. The Law on State Enterprises, which came into force on 1 January 1988 was also a good example of inconsistency. The positive aspect of the Law was that it allowed for the creation of many new kinds of enterprises, but it was again 'a halfway attempt at economic reform, leaving the economy neither plan nor market. Officially, compulsory plan targets were abolished; in reality, they remained in water-downed form.... Rather than paving the way for a market economy, the Law on State Enterprises encouraged manipulation of the old rules.'[59] There were also some half-hearted reform attempts in the area of foreign trade. In December 1988, a decree of the USSR Council of Ministers decentralized foreign trade activities but only to a very limited extent and without eliminating the state monopoly of foreign trade. Imports and exports remained centrally controlled through administrative instruments, tariffs were not used either for import nor for export regulation. Rules were further loosened on joint ventures with foreign participation, but they still remained subject to special permit. Although a currency retention scheme was also introduced, and a currency and tariff reform was envisaged, hundreds of currency coefficients were still used for the distribution of export earnings between exporters and the state. There was no economic relationship between foreign and domestic prices; a substantial portion of imports were subsidized. There were no comprehensive plans for the reform of the CMEA either.[60] In 1990 and 1991, the economy of the Soviet Union was already in a state of collapse. Within this two year period GDP declined by 8 per cent and inflation in 1991, due to an ill-fated price liberalization, reached 100 per cent; the budget recorded an enormous deficit, exceeding 20 per cent of GDP. Under Gorbachev, the economy did not become more efficient. Improvements in standard of living were bought at the expense of the central budget; a substantial contributory factor to the rapidly expanding chaos.

Despite the inconsistent reform measures, economic thinking did make a big step forward in the Soviet Union during these years. Many of the best economists in the country were involved in the preparation of different economic reform programmes which were debated publicly. In October 1989, Abalkin tabled his economic reform package, which emphasized the establishment of a market economy; the liberalization of prices; competition among economic units; the introduction of a convertible currency and the creation of a stock market. In early 1990, G. Yavlinsky and two other young economists, inspired by the success of the 'Polish shock therapy' presented a more radical programme, called the The '400–day programme' for transition of the Soviet Union to a market economy. The plan included rapid price liberalization, economic stabilization measures and large-scale privatization through sales. Based on an agreement between Gorbachev and Yeltsin, a group of economists under the leadership of S. Shatalin prepared another similarly radical programme for economic transition, the '500–day plan'. But by the end of 1990, there was increasing evidence that Gorbachev and the Communist Party was not in favour of any large-scale privatization, or any radical economic reforms. Gorbachev and his entourage continued to believe in central planning. They were in favour of movements toward a market economy only within the framework of a planned economy. In October 1990, Gorbachev rejected Shatalin's '500–day plan'.[61] It was correctly noted that

'After October 1990, everything began to fall apart, and Gorbachev once again embraced the old communist establishment.'[62]

The different reform plans were not implemented, but still played a vital role because they focused the attention of political leaders and society as a whole to some basic economic problems the resolution of which was an absolute precondition for any meaningful social progress in the country.[63] Many elements from these transformation programmes were used in Russia, after the dissolution of the Soviet Union, when the implementation of radical reforms were put on the agenda.

Real political reforms

Gorbachev will probably be remembered by history not for his hesitant economic half measures but for the domestic and foreign policy changes which occurred during his years in power. In the area of political freedoms, the new election law liberalized election rules, without allowing the establishment of competing political parties, however.[64] Laws adopted in this period introduced elements of freedom and democracy to public life which had been completely absent in the previous seven decades. These freedoms prepared the way for the further development and democratization of Russian political institutions and the adoption of radical market economy measures.[65] The new laws brought the public's attention to the importance of individual rights and freedoms and thus played an important role in the development of the Russian constitutional system. It was rightly stated that, the very fact that issues related to individual liberty were debated, gave people a sense of real freedom for the first time, and that 'Freedom became a norm that could no longer be denied them.'[66] This new approach to individual liberty was clearly expressed by the massive popular support given to Yeltsin who defended these rights against the puschists in August 1991.

It would be really very difficult to overestimate the importance of the Gorbachev's policies which allowed countries in Central and Eastern Europe to take their fate into their own hands. As a result of them, both the Warsaw Pact and the CMEA ceased to exist in 1991. When the danger of a nuclear war between the superpowers disappeared, substantial defence cuts could be made by the Soviet Union. The revision of the Union Treaty, which was initiated by Gorbachev, was also of outstanding historical importance, triggering a series of events including the signature of the Belovezhsky Agreement, on 8 December 1991, by the leaders of Belarus, Russia and Ukraine, which resulted in the dissolution of the Soviet Union and the creation of new states from the former Soviet republics.

The lack of legal and institutional changes

During the long decades of dictatorship in the Soviet Union, the country became a legal and institutional wasteland. Soviet laws soon drove out the old Russian legal system, which were also underdeveloped in themselves. In the economic sphere, administrative hierarchies replaced commercial relationships between enterprises. Plan targets or state orders dictated what enterprises had to produce and to whom the goods should be delivered. Relationships between enterprises were regulated not by contracts but by administrative orders. Civil law therefore had practically no place at all in inter-enterprise relationships. The economy-related judicial system was also transformed completely. Special administrative bodies were created for taking decisions in legal disputes between enterprises. Decisions were taken to promote the fulfilment of plans. And, of course, institutions related to traditional contract enforcement, competition or bankruptcy lost their role and disappeared, together with the appropriate expertise. Bank and credit relations were victim to the same fate. The Soviet system did not need real financial institutions. The economy became totally isolated from the outside world through the planning system, and the state's foreign trade and currency monopolies. Three generations grew up in this anti-market, anti-law environment. One can state fairly, that by the 1980s the economic, legal and human infrastructure of the Soviet Union was totally incompatible with the requirements of a market economy.

Under Gorbachev no general legal reforms were carried out. In the area of public law, a clear separation between legislative and executive power was lacking; serious constitutional problems could be raised in respect of many legal rules and decisions. Gorbachev himself amassed increasing power to rule by executive decree. This power was first given to Gorbachev for 18 months in September 1990, but was expanded and later made permanent. The Soviet Union, Gorbachev said in an interview, 'is not ready for the procedures of a law-based state.'[67] The reason for the neglect of legal reforms, including the adoption of a new Constitution, was probably that the leadership felt a more developed legal system could prevent the introduction of necessary reform measures in the form of decrees. Another reason was that Gorbachev did not really understand the importance of constitutionalism and the wider implications of the concept of the state of law. It was rightly noted that for him 'democracy and constitutionalism were not ends in themselves but simply means to the ends of economic reform.'[68] Neither did Gorbachev understand the role of the civil society and consequently had no programme on its development.

Corruption and the strengthening of the mafia were also facilitated by Gorbachev's inconsistent policies. Prices of many goods, which were easy to sell in the home market or abroad, were strictly controlled. Refined oil was 146 times and, crude oil some 100 times cheaper in Russia than on the world market.[69] As party and policy control weakened, it became easy for mafias to get rich overnight.

Radical economic reforms in Russia

After the August 1991 coup, it became clear that the days of the Soviet Union were numbered. Russia had inherited economic chaos from the Soviet Union: real GDP fell approximately 12 per cent; and the budget deficit reached 26 per cent of GDP. Foreign trade contracted even more steeply: in volume terms, Russian exports declined by 29 per cent, while imports by 46 per cent in 1991, compared to 1990. Consumer price inflation increased from 4 per cent in October 1991 to 9 per cent in the next month and 12 per cent in December. In 1991, the price index for consumer goods and services was 89 per cent higher than the year before. In the same 12 months real wages fell by 12 per cent. Goods were disappearing from the shelves and queues outside shops kept growing. It was obvious that the old economic system had broken down and central planning could not fulfil its economic functions any more. At the same time, again due to the inconsistent reforms of the Gorbachev area, the market economy, or even its basic elements, were still far from being established. The disintegration of the Soviet Union made the economic situation even worse, as economic ties between its constituent republics were severely disrupted. The need for urgent and fundamental changes in the economy was supreme.

Reform economist, G. Yavlinsky and others, realized that no consistent market economy reforms could be expected from Gorbachev. They turned away from him and put their trust in his adversary, Boris

Yeltsin who, in May 1990, became Chairman of Russia's Supreme Soviet and was elected President of Russia in June 1991. After the August coup, Yeltsin accepted the idea of a radical economic reform programme for Russia. It was a surprise when Yeltsin turned for advice for Yegor Gaidar, a young and inexperienced economist. The reason behind the decision was probably that Gaidar, foreseeing the inevitable dissolution of the Soviet Union, had formulated a reform programme for an independent Russia, and not for the Soviet Union, and this coincided with Yeltsin's aspirations. According to reports, Yeltsin and Gaidar had not even met each other before the August 1991 putsch.[70] But reportedly, in his 28 October 1991 reform speech before Russia's Congress of People's Deputies, Yeltsin included many of Gaidar's ideas.[71] The speech announced radical economic reforms, covering price liberalization, privatization, and tight monetary and fiscal policies. He also requested additional powers for the implementation of the reforms. Both the reform programme and the request for additional powers were approved on 1 November 1991. With this decision the Russian President was granted the power to rule largely by decree for one year. Unexpectedly, Gaidar, without any administrative experience, was soon appointed minister of finance in the new reform-minded Russian government.[72]

Gaidar's reform programme never took any clear formulation and it was not published. It was worked out by a number of reform economists with the support of foreign advisers.[73] The original Gaidar programme, 'Stabilization and Reform', which was an unofficial working paper, proposed gradual stabilization and liberalization to be implemented during a one year period.[74] The programme was a problem-oriented document with little emphasis on general political and economic principles.

The isolation of the reformers from the population was further aggravated by the lack of any government campaign to explain the reforms, gather popular support for them, or help overcome the disillusion and apathy of the Russian people after the unsuccessful reform efforts of Gorbachev. The foreign advisers were not satisfied with the programme either, they criticised it and 'urged as comprehensive a big bang as possible, including wider simultaneous price liberalization, stricter monetary policy, more liberalization of foreign trade, early unification of the exchange rate, full convertibility on current account, and greater efforts to mobilize international financing.'[75]

Introduction of the stabilization and reform programme in early 1992

In January 1992, after a short period of preparation, the new reform government launched a comprehensive programme, which was worked out together with the IMF, aimed at reconstructing the troubled Russian economy. The main elements of the stabilization programme included the following:

- the goal of reducing the very large combined budget deficit of Russia and the former USSR to zero in the first quarter of 1992;
- large cuts in social programmes, military procurement and investment;
- the creation of a value-added tax, set at 28 per cent, and an increase in payroll taxes;
- sharp cuts in the money supply and the volume of credit to be implemented by the Russian Central Bank.

From November 1991, a number of presidential decrees were adopted with the objective of laying down the fundamentals of a consistent market economy. These decrees covered such important areas as the reorganization of the structure of the Russian government; liberalization of foreign economic activity; abolition of wage limits; regulation of exports of oil and oil products; reform of government financing; price liberalization; land reform; regulation of trade with other CIS countries; privatization; introduction of excise duties; licensing and quotas for exports and imports; taxation; currency circulation and customs duties for imported goods.[76]

Liberalization of prices

The liberalization of prices was considered as a key constituent part of the Russian reform programme. At the beginning of 1992, a government resolution ordered all enterprises, except those which remained under state control, to free their prices. The prices of about 10 per cent of basic consumer items (such as bread, milk, matches, salt, vodka, electricity charges, housing rentals) remained subject to government control.[77] But even prices under government control were raised from three to five times. Twenty per cent of producer prices (electricity, fuels, precious metals and freight tariffs) also stayed controlled. However, many oil products were not under price control, resulting in windfall profits for the oil processing industry. The production of certain items enjoyed government subsidies if restrictions made production unprofitable.[78] And unlike a number of other transition economies, no wage control schemes were introduced in Russia because the government considered such policies neither feasible nor effective due to the specific features of Russian industrial relations.[79]

It is difficult to estimate the overall degree of price controls because local authorities frequently imposed them on such items as staple food or transport tariffs, often together with additional restrictions on exports across *oblast* borders.[80] In some cases, price controls were introduced by the organs of the State Committee for Anti-monopoly Policy. In March 1995, many price controls were eliminated, but local governments continued to regulate or subsidize the prices of a few staple foods.[81]

The liberalization and deregulation programme was also applied to domestic distribution and road transport, but not to rail transport.[82] The role of former distribution systems for producer goods, the centralized allocation system with the State Planning Committee (Gosplan) and the State Committee for Material and Technical Supplies (Gossnab) was diminished substantially, but some state distribution units remained in existence. In the first half of 1992, purchase through state orders reached only about 40 per cent of the production of state-owned enterprises, much less than planned. Little remained of the system of state orders by the end of 1993. However, a number of monopolies dealing with gasoline, natural gas, grain, timber and interstate trade with CIS countries survived.[83]

In January 1992, the presidential decree on freedom of trade, liberalized practically all trade activities. Its purpose was to enhance competition in retail trade. Within a very short period of time, Russian streets became full of private street traders who offered anything for which they could find demand. But the positive reaction of the public soon turned into dissatisfaction due to the public disorder street trading caused and the questionable quality of the products sold. There was also a widespread view that street traders were not really necessary, because they just resold items at a higher price which had been purchased in state-owned shops. Soon after the liberalization of retail trade, authorities took a restrictive approach against it because they 'did not receive any revenue, legal or illegal, from the disorganized street trade.'[84] In Moscow, the city authorities regulated street trade at the end of April 1992. In June, a presidential decree also introduced restrictions. Street traders were obliged to sell their products from kiosks. These restrictions made it easier for organized crime to take almost total control of retail trade in big cities. The demand for regulating street trade, however, came not only from people who 'did not understand that efficient allocation of goods was a value in itself' or from bribe-hungry officials and conservative politicians,[85] it also came from new private shop-owners. They complained, rightly, that street traders constituted unfair competition as they easily avoided tax payments and did not maintain costly overheads.

Monetary and fiscal policy[86]

Russian reformers wanted to achieve stabilization through a combination of massive fiscal adjustment measures and restrictive monetary and credit policy. Budget expenditure was to be reduced substantially, particularly in the areas of subsidies, military spending and centralized investments. Budget revenues were expected to remain level, mainly due to the strengthening and broadening of the tax base through the imposition of VAT and taxes on energy exports. The objective was to have a balanced budget by the first quarter of 1992.

   At the beginning of the implementation of the reform programme, the Russian government implemented a restrictive monetary policy. Between December 1991 and April 1992, the consumer price index, mainly due to price liberalization, increased by 655 per cent. In the same period, total credit emission increased much less, by only 131 per cent and cash issue by only 91 per cent. 'The drastic fall in the real supply of credit was obtained initially through overall credit limits (a 15 per cent ceiling on the increase of credit stock in the first quarter) and later through increases in the basic interest rate – from 2–9 per cent to 20 per cent in January, 50 per cent in March, and to 80 per cent in May.'[87] The budget deficit, due to cuts in government expenditure, was reduced to 3.5 per cent of GDP by the end of the first quarter of 1992. It was rightly noted, 'In a normal market economy, a financial squeeze of that magnitude would immediately have driven many firms out of business and provoked large rises in unemployment.... In Russia, however, it quickly turned out that the bankruptcy laws and the disciplines of contract enforcement left much to be desired.'[88] At the time of the these reform measures, Russia did not have bankruptcy legislation. (The Law on Corporate

Insolvency came into force in March 1993. But even years later, the Russian bankruptcy law was considered ineffective.) In addition, it was well known that the 'ability of courts to enforce debt collection in practice' was critical.[89] The government's inability to eliminate loss-making firms quickly taught state-owned enterprises that non-payments did not necessarily result in bankruptcy procedures. This fact largely contributed to the radical increase of inter-enterprise credits.

Enterprises reacted to restrictive monetary policies differently than expected. The liquidity shortage, which was aggravated by the unexpectedly high inflation, lead to massive non-payments and rapidly increasing indebtedness of enterprises. Within three months, from the end of 1991, inter-enterprise arrears increased from rouble 40 billion to 751 billion, more than twice of the amount of credit emission by the banking system. For similar reasons, arrears in cash wage payments increased to 8 per cent of total monthly income of the population. The non-payment crises, of course, were further deepened by the absence of appropriate institutional infrastructure.

The most important change in the fiscal area was the elimination of the traditional socialist type turnover tax and the introduction of value-added tax in January1992. Until December 1992, the VAT rates were 15 and 28 per cent. One of the main reasons for introducing the VAT was that it provided a reliable source of government revenue with limited possibilities for tax avoidance and tax evasion. The introduced profit tax rate was 32 per cent, while individual income tax rates ranged between 0 and 40 per cent. The rate of the social security tax was 38 per cent.[90] By that time it was already clear that the absence of a professional tax administration made the realization of the tax collection objectives of the Gaidar government unlikely.[91]

Reform of the banking system

In the Soviet Union a two-tier banking system was created in 1987 as part of the perestroika reforms. In December 1991, new laws on the central bank and commercial banks were adopted. Due to very liberal prudential regulations and weak banking supervision, which became one of the contributory factors to the weakness of the whole sector, the number of commercial banks increased sharply. By the mid-1990s, the number well exceeded 2000. However, in November 1993 tight restrictions were imposed on foreign banks. The aggregate capital of these banks was not allowed to exceed 12 per cent of the total capital of the domestic banking system. The major problem of the Russian banking system was that from the start commercial banks did not become involved in restructuring and investment activities. They concentrated on more profitable business such as keeping a high share of zero-interest deposits in a time of very high inflation, or later, buying high-yielding state securities.[92]

Causes of high inflation

Inflation was miscalculated by the government. In January 1992, the consumer price index rose by 245 per cent as compared with December 1991. The 500 per cent inflation envisaged for 1992 was already surpassed in March (618 per cent). Experts identified a number of economic factors behind this. These included the existence of a highly monopolized and specialized anti-competition market structure and the extremely large size of Russian enterprises, a heritage from the Soviet planned economy.[93] It was mainly due to the high degree of monopolization of the Russian market that enterprise profits, despite drastic cuts in monetary supply, increased considerably in the first stage of the 1992 stabilization programme.[94] The very low level of competition in the Russian economy was aggravated by the weakness of imports caused by the restricted convertibility, the existence of multiple exchange rates, an extremely depreciated market exchange rate of the rouble *vis-à-vis* convertible currencies. The absurd degree of the depreciation of the rouble was indicated by the fact that prices of traded goods were, at the market exchange rate, only about one-twentieth of world prices,[95] and in December 1991, the average monthly wage in Russia, calculated on similar basis, was US$6.[96] Depreciation provided effective protection against imports for the still state-owned domestic industry, which enjoyed a monopolistic situation in most cases.

   High inflation was also due, to a considerable extent, to the Russian trade surplus with other CIS countries.

> Lack of regulations to limit technical credits in bilateral trade, coupled with practically unrestricted possibilities for other republics' central banks to issue credit to local banks and enterprises, resulted in large Russian trade surpluses, which were financed through an accumulation of claims on the correspondent accounts held by other republics' central banks in the Russian central bank. The share of interstate payments in the monetary

base of the Central Bank of Russia (CBR) increased from nil at the end of 1991 to 13.6 per cent by the end of the first quarter, and to 29.2 per cent by the end of the first half of 1992.[97]

Liberalization of foreign trade

The reform of the foreign trade sector and the integration of the national economy into the world economy were vital issues for all transition economies which wanted to end their decades long isolation from world markets. Russia's foreign trade was in crisis in 1990 and 1991, with both exports and imports declining sharply. The institutional system of Russian foreign trade was inefficient, obsolete and contradictory to the basic objectives of economic reform which called for the replacement of administrative trade controls with price mechanism devices, including the introduction of a tariff system.

Presidential Decree No. 213 of 15 November 1991 'On Liberalization of Foreign Economic Activity on the Territory of the Russian Federation' eliminated the state's foreign trade monopoly. All economic entities, irrespective of their form of ownership, were given the right to carry out foreign economic activities. Exports of 'strategically important raw materials' were limited to entities specifically registered with the Ministry of Foreign Economic Relations (MFER).[98]

At the beginning of the reform process, Russia, due to different distortions and supply constraints in its domestic market, maintained a complex system of export regulations. Beyond the bureaucratic (and corrupt) system of centralized exporters, the more important export items were subject to quotas and licensing. In early 1992, these items, which accounted for about 70 per cent of all exports, included oil, oil products, gas, coal, metals, fertilizers, various chemical products, timber, fish and weapons. In addition, these products were also subject to export tariffs. The reason behind the simultaneous application of administrative and tariff controls was the enormous difference between domestic Russian prices and world prices, and the determination of the government to maintain a minimal supply of basic items to the domestic market.[99] It was obvious that low domestic energy prices benefited exporters who could export such products with substantial profit. Therefore, the main purpose of export licensing was price control. The level of export tariffs, 20 to 30 per cent at the beginning, was determined as a percentage of world market prices, to avoid under-priced customs declarations. Export tariff rates were frequently changed.[100]

The sophisticated export control system could not be implemented properly due to the chaotic situation in the administration. Rampant corruption was facilitated by uncontrolled discretionary power enjoyed by the administration. Auctioning of export quotas could not be introduced because of the resistance of the corrupt beneficiaries of the discretionary system. Peter Aven, Russia's reformist minister of foreign economic relations, commenting on large administrative controls, stated: 'One important lesson can be drawn from this experience, namely, that any obstacle to economic activity, especially one which assumes the existence of a discretionary choice, will be circumvented in Russia, and therefore this country has to be more liberal than any other.'[101] A. Åslund generalized this dictum by stating '. . . strong states can liberalize slowly, weak states cannot.'[102]

At the beginning of the reform period, Russia's import regime was very simple. The government, to facilitate import competition, suspended application of customs tariffs on imports with effect from 15 January 1992. As a result, neither customs duties, nor other levies, quotas or licensing were imposed on imports. But the extremely undervalued rouble provided a very substantial protection to the domestic economy against import competition. In July 1992, under the pressure of the industrial lobby and also for fiscal reasons, a unified 5 per cent import tariff was introduced, which was raised to 15 per cent in September. The diversification of the import tariffs started in 1993, but the problem was that 'Nobody could tell which industries actually needed tariff protection.'[103] As we will see, this situation has not changed since, which explains the frequent changes in Russian import tariffs and other elements of the foreign trade regulatory system. Since the beginning of 1993, a number of goods have been subject to excise taxes. Similarly, the value-added tax was also imposed on imported products.

Behind the introduction of the tariff system and the determination of export and import tariff rates, fiscal considerations played an important role. At the beginning of the reform period, state revenues from export–import activities accounted for about 20 per cent of all budgetary revenues. It should be noted, however, that exemptions from export–import duties were quite substantial.

Currency regulation

In November 1991, Russia introduced, through a presidential decree, radical changes in the foreign exchange system which included a drastic devaluation of the rouble and a freely floating inter-bank exchange rate for all non-government foreign exchange transactions. The rouble could not be fixed or pegged to the US$ or other convertible currency, which could have served as a nominal anchor during the transition period, as it would have needed substantial currency reserves. Lack of these reserves coupled with the IMF's decision not to provide Russia with stabilization funds, meant this avenue was closed.[104] The multiple currency coefficients were abolished. Exporters were obliged to surrender 40 per cent of their convertible currency earnings at a fixed exchange rate, which was about 50 per cent lower than the auction rate. An additional 10 per cent of earnings had to be sold to banks at the auction exchange rate. These new measures were a substantial change from the earlier period when the purchasing of hard currency for imports was difficult, and its rules lacked transparency. In 1991, due to the artificial exchange rate, import subsidies reached about 20 per cent of the GNP.

The exchange rate for almost all currency transactions was unified in July 1992. From that time the auction rate applied to currency surrender, currency auctions and currency purchases for imports.[105] Twenty per cent of convertible currency earnings had to be sold through the currency auctions and 30 per cent through the Central Bank. Special exchange rates were applied to centralized imports with the objective to subsidize imports through the exchange rate. The coverage of centralized imports decreased during the second half of 1992. By the end of the year only a small number of food items still belonged to this category.

The early reform of currency regulations resulted in a *de facto* current account currency convertibility for residents: a drastic change from the earlier regime under which all currency transactions were strictly centralized and all violations carried the risk of criminal prosecution.

The end of the rouble zone

After the dissolution of the Soviet Union CIS members could not reach agreement on economic reforms or economic policy. As the Soviet republics became independent countries, trade among them became foreign trade. But because of the collapse of central planning, the lack of any agreement on economic and trade reforms and the absence of co-ordination between the newly established countries, former trade relations were disrupted causing substantial chaos in all the economies concerned. New trade barriers were introduced, but in the institutional vacuum which followed the collapse of the command economy, barter became widespread.

The only common, trade-related institution which survived from Soviet times was the rouble and the rouble zone. In the former Soviet republics, a *de facto* monetary union existed until the end of 1991. This was replaced by separate, but interdependent, national currency systems. CIS member countries tried but failed to reach consensus on the reform of the rouble zone. The main problem with the rouble zone was that the central bank of each country produced its own non-cash rouble to finance trade among CIS countries. As Russia was a net creditor with all countries, the CBR financed the bilateral payments deficit of other CIS countries *vis-à-vis* Russia. The resulting transfers to other former Soviet republics were some 8 per cent of Russian GDP in 1992.[106] Russia, for obvious reasons, wanted to maintain one monetary authority with technical control over issuing of money. The other CIS countries, while agreeing on credit limits, insisted on keeping their own central banks. The other main contention was the issue of voting rights. Russia wanted GDP-related votes, which was not acceptable to the other countries.[107] Failure to reform the rouble zone, and other developments, such as the shortage of cash roubles, accelerated the establishment of national currencies. By the end of 1992, the Baltic states and Ukraine completed the process of separating their monetary systems from the rouble zone, thus the rouble remained in unrestricted circulation only in Russia and in some Asian republics.[108] The rouble zone was finished in July 1993, when the CBR introduced a currency reform which required all previously issued cash to be exchanged for new Russian roubles, at Russian banks.[109] Thus, after the currency reform, 'relations with CIS countries were no longer a strain on monetary policy, although the bilateral payments imbalances remain, and most CIS countries are unable to settle the debts that arise.'[110]

Reaction of economic units and society to radical reforms

As a result of the liberalization measures, the situation on the market of consumer goods improved and most shortages disappeared. In February and March 1992, food items became more readily available compared to the end of 1991, but shortages of important products could still be observed in many cities.[111] The initial reaction of state-owned enterprises to the drastic changes in the general economic environment was different than expected. Supply responses were weak and restructuring in the enterprise sector failed to start. Instead, production declined steeply and inter-enterprise debts grew as enterprises tried to protect employment and wages. Rapid adjustment to the new economic environment was hindered by the absence of an adequate market-related institutional system which included modern banking and financial services, sales and purchasing networks, insurance and legal services. In 1992, output fell by 20 per cent, the level of consumer prices rose by 26 times and trades and payments relations with the former Soviet republics became chaotic. The drastic economic decline led to growing social and ethnic tensions and diminished job security. Criminality started to rise sharply.

As a result of sharp deterioration in the economic and social situation, industrial lobbies of state-owned enterprises, through the use of Parliament, exerted more and more pressures on the government to soften macroeconomic policies. Workers also protested against the worsening working and living conditions. The government, which had no strong political support in the Parliament, gave in to these pressures in early summer 1992. The softening of the stabilization policy took the form of tolerating increasing tax arrears and the expansion of soft commercial credits which amounted to the granting of subsidies. In protest against mounting pressures to relax financial and monetary policies, the chairman of CBR, Mr Matyukin stepped down in June 1992. He was replaced by Mr Gerashchenko who advocated a far more active lending policy towards enterprises in financial trouble. This was in clear defiance of the restrictive monetary and fiscal policies worked out in accordance with IMF stabilization guidelines, which were approved by the government on 30 June 1992. As a result of the new policy, CBR loans to commercial banks increased sharply, while the total amount of credits growing by 32 per cent between the end of May and the end of June. In July, the overall credit stock increased by 65 per cent and cash emission by 42 per cent. This trend continued throughout the whole year. Interest rates, in real terms, became negative, as they did not adequately reflect the rise in inflation. Negative real interest rates helped the survival of debtors, which were mainly over-staffed state-owned enterprises with totally obsolete production structures. But it also wiped out savings and destroyed financial disciplines.[112] Another consequence was that the federal budget deficit, because it financed the interest rate differentials for concessionary credits, exceeded 13 per cent of GDP by August. The value of the rouble plummeted against convertible currencies and inflation accelerated again, reaching 900–1000 per cent annually in the last quarter of 1992.[113] Capital flight and dollarization of the economy also gained momentum.

Despite the relaxation of financial policies, the decline in industrial output continued, even accelerated. Enterprises used soft loans to repay debts and to hedge against inflation. But accelerating inflation led to a new wave of enterprise indebtedness, non-payments and a further expansion of credit.[114] The economic environment did not impose a hard budgetary constraint on economic units. In 1992, the financial position of Russian enterprises, despite the catastrophic economic situation, deteriorated only marginally and were much better, at least on paper, than in other countries. By the second half of 1992 it became clear that that 'the attempt to solve the payments crises through large-scale credit expansion clearly had failed: the only tangible result was runaway inflation, free fall of the rouble and the continuous recession in the production sector.'[115] The failure of the Gaidar programme became evident. Leftist and communist forces in Parliament, which were elected in 1990, expressed severe criticism about the social costs of the shock therapy. Though employment was falling more slowly than industrial output, average real wages fell by 18 per cent in 1992 and hardship increased for a substantial propor- tion of the population, widening inequality.[116] Representatives of industrial complexes pointed to the danger of collapse in different sectors of manufacturing due to the macroeconomic restrictions and new relative prices. 'Some even suspected that one of the purposes of the programme was to destroy the high-technology sectors of the Russian economy and to force unilateral disarmament of Russia's military forces.'[117]

Concern was also expressed over the internal inconsistency of the programme and the lack of institutional support for the reform pro- cess. But the most important factor was the political weakness and isolation of the Gaidar government. The reform economists and polit- icians did not enjoy either the support of any powerful political parties nor the population in general. The voice of the critics in the Parliament became stronger and stronger. At the end of the year, the Congress of People's Deputies, signalling the growing ideological differences between the Parliament and the presidency over economic policy, refused to extend Yeltsin's temporary powers and, on 12 December 1992, forced him to dismiss Gaidar as acting prime minister. Two days later, with the massive support of the industrial lobby, Yeltsin appointed Viktor Chernomyrdin as Russia's new prime minister.

Unsuccessful attempts to achieve macroeconomic stability (1993–94)

The new Russian government, led by Chernomyrdin, announced an ambitious programme to combat inflation. It did not deviate substantially from the strategy followed by the Gaidar team, but it drew some lessons from the mistakes they made. The main macroeconomic tasks defined by the programme were to fight inflation and stabilize public finances. The target was to lower the budget deficit to 5 per cent of GDP and the monthly rate of inflation to 5 per cent by the end of 1993. These goals were to be achieved through measures such as substantial rises in interest rates, the introduction of noninflationary ways of deficit financing and restrictions on credit emissions. International financial institutions welcomed the programme.

The CBR and industrial circles opposed the policy of credit restriction. The new reformist finance minister, B Fedorov, used the Commission of Credit Policy to control the volume of credits. The government requested the CBR to increase the refinancing interest rate from 80 to 100 per cent in March and 140 per cent in April, which it rejected, even though the annual rate of inflation was running at 1000–1500 per cent. CBR officials took the view that inflation was independent of monetary policy and additional credits served to stimulate production rather than demand. Later the CBR conceded to government pressure and the interest rate was raised to 100 per cent at the end of March and ceilings were established for CBR credits to commercial banks, restricting credit expansion to 30 per cent in the second quarter of 1993. In May 1993, a joint 'Declaration on the Economic Policy of the Government and the Central Bank of Russia' was signed by prime minister Chernomyrdin and the chairman of the CBR, Gerashchenko. The document specified that the CBR rate would be no lower than 7 percentage points below the interest rate prevailing on the interbank market.[118]

On 25 April 1993, a referendum expressed support for economic reforms and the president himself. This supported the government's fight for additional increases in central bank rates, which were still negative in real terms. As a result of the Government's pressure, central bank interest rates were increased several times in the second half of the year.[119] By November 1993, they became positive.

The budget improved slightly in 1993. Tax collection remained a problem, which reflected both the weakness of the federal institutions in this field and the prevailing morality. If tax income increased somewhat, it was due to VAT being extended to imports and some additional levies and excise taxes being imposed. On the expenditure side, the substantial cut in coal subsidies should be mentioned as a consequence of price liberalization in the sector. Import subsidies were also reduced substantially.[120] These measures contributed to keeping the budget deficit within the limits agreed on with the IMF. In 1993, the government for the first time issued government bonds to finance the budget deficit and cover internal debt. In 1993, Russia had a high rate of inflation, but it escaped hyperinflation because the growth of wages lagged behind the growth of prices; the contraction of real credit continued in 1993 and, due to the underdeveloped banking system, 'massive injections of CBR credits into the banking sector were not fully transmitted to the enterprise sector, because the banks preferred to increase their investments in other assets, primary in foreign exchange holdings.[121] This, of course, further decreased the amount of money available to the business sector for the purpose of restructuring.

The fight between Parliament and the presidency

The different political priorities of the presidency, the reform-minded government and the Parliament, which was opposed to the radical transformation of the country, manifested itself in constant and unfruitful debates in Parliament and led to a *de facto* dual power. The antagonistic nature of the differences came to the surface during the second half of 1993 in a brutal way. In the economic area, controversies concentrated around the budget and the restrictive measures proposed by the government and the IMF. At the end of May, the government and, under the government's weight, the CBR signed an agreement with the IMF imposing specified limits on the growth of monetary, credit and budgetary flows which led to the release of the first tranche of credits within the framework of the Systemic Transformation Facility (STF) of US$3 billion. Half of this amount was made available for Russia immediately after the signature of the agreement, while the second tranche was to be disbursed only after the results of the new policy were known. The agreement provided, *inter alia*, for the reduction of the government budget to 8.9 per cent of GDP in the first half of 1993 and to 8.3 per cent for the whole year of 1993. The Parliament was opposed these restrictive measures, rejected the budget prepared by the government and proposed an increase of the planned deficit from 10.4 per cent to more than 20 per cent of GDP. The President vetoed this budgetary proposal, but the Parliament overruled the presidential veto by qualified majority. On 21 September, the President, in Decree no. 1400, dissolved the Supreme Soviet and the Congress of People's Deputies and called for new elections and a referendum on a new draft constitution. He also suspended parts of the Constitution and enjoined the constitutional Court from meeting before the new parliamentary elections. Nevertheless, the Constitutional Court, without the participation of the judges who complied with Yeltsin's Decree, held an emergency meeting, declared Decree no. 1400 unconstitutional and called on the Parliament to impeach the President. The Parliament did not accept its dissolution and under the leadership of Vice-President Alexander Rutskoi and the Speaker of the Parliament Ruslan Khasbulatov an armed uprising was organized which occupied the Parliament building. After heated street battles, on 4 October 1993, special military forces launched a massive artillery attack against the occupied White House and stormed the building. The rebellion was soon over. More than 100 people died.

Immediately after the dissolution of the Parliament, the government, with Gaidar who rejoined it as deputy prime minister on 18 September, took advantage of the changed power relations by implementing some reform-oriented measures. In the absence of a Parliament the President ruled by decree between 21 September and 12 January 1994. On 25 September, credits subsidized with low interest rates were abolished; measures of a deregulatory nature were taken in agriculture, prices of bread, grain and baby food were liberalized and food procurement by the state was stopped. Budgetary discipline was also strengthened. 'Reformers made a new attempt to oust the conservative chairman of the CBR, but Chernomyrdin saved him. Nevertheless, Gerashchenko adjusted to the reformist pressure.'[122]

Economic policies after the no confidence vote for radical reformers in December 1993

On 12 December 1993, political parties which were in favour of a fast and radical transformation of the Russian economy and society suffered a major setback. With an election turnout of about 55 per cent of the voters, the winners were the Liberal Democratic Party and the Communist Party, together with the similarly oriented Agrarian Party. The communist and nationalist block received about 40 per cent of the votes, while the liberal parties got 30 per cent. The so-called 'centrist' parties took the rest of the seats. As a result of the changed power relations in Parliament, Gaidar and Fedorov resigned from the government in early 1994. Of the reform-minded politicians only Chubais became a member of Chernomyrdin's new government, as deputy prime minsiter. The other members of the government were known mainly from their close relationships with different industrial and agricultural lobbies.

On 12 December, voters also adopted by a small margin the draft of the Constitution proposed by Yeltsin. The new Constitution gave to the President larger powers. It provided that in the absence of laws the decrees signed by the president had the force of law, with the constraint that the Duma could supersede such decrees by laws. (The Federal Assembly was constituted of two houses: the State Duma with 450 elected members and the Federation Council, with 178 members.) From the beginning of 1994, major economic policies took the form of presidential decrees or government decisions. The Constitutional Court, which could judge the constitutionality of a disputed piece of legislation, remained inoperative during 1994, because the President and the Duma could not agree on how it should be composed. The President-driven legal environment, which followed from the new Constitution, did not provide a stable basis for business. The uncertain legal situation was made worse by serious problems in implementing the rules, due to institutional weaknesses, inadequate public service, corruption and the growing power of the mafia.

The newly elected Duma was not active in the area of economic legislation until late 1994. By the end of 1993, the CBR adopted a restrictive monetary policy which, after some hesitation, was also followed by the new Chernomyrdin government. In the light of three years of stabilization failures, it was largely agreed by both politicians and industrialists that hyperinflation was to be avoided and economic stability was absolutely necessary. In 1994, soft credits to different economic sectors were no longer given directly by the CBR. Credits which were maintained had to be part of the budget.[123]

Fiscal problems

There were substantial problems with the budget, which was accepted by the Duma only in June 1994. The government raised the share of the consolidated state budget in GDP, which included the federal and the regional budgets. It quickly turned out that the implementation of the move was not feasible as the proposed 5 per cent increase of state revenues was impossible. Tax collection became a serious problem in 1994 and later. The total tax revenue as a share of GDP, as in other transition economies, continued to decline in 1994.[124] However, Central European countries and Estonia managed to stop the decline, but Russia and some other former Soviet republics could not.[125]

The reasons for weak tax collection were many. They included the size of the shadow economy, approximately one third of total GDP; the decreasing number of large state-owned industrial enterprises which could be taxed relatively easily; the growth of the emerging private sector, consisting mainly of small enteprises which, as a rule, tried to avoid paying taxes; the large number of, and very high, tax rates; the inefficient Russian tax collection system, which included the frequent reluctance of regional tax authorities to transfer the full amount of taxes collected to the federal authorities; corruption and illegal confiscatory extortion which led to the development of sophisticated tax-evasion methods. The numerous tax exemptions, often created by presidential decrees, also played a role. Many exemptions covered the energy sector; companies were exempted from the export tax on oil, for example. 'The exemptions have typically been granted in order to influence the behaviour of the company concerned, for example to persuade an energy company not to take proceedings against its debtors.'[126] It should also not be forgotten that the strict monetary policy being followed demonetized the economy, substantially facilitating, even forcing the wide-spread use of barter, which also made a big contribution to poor tax collection records. Loss of revenue in 1994 due to tax and tariff exemptions was estimated to amount to 1.5 per cent of GDP or 10 per cent of actual revenue to the federal budget. Importantly, the loss of revenue and the deficit were concentrated in the federal budget, while 'sub-federal budgets tended to be in broad balance, or even small surplus, in aggregate.'[127]

In light of declining budget revenues, the government had to sequester expenditures aggressively. The implementation of the reduction was subject to criticism, as the ministry of finance simply refused previously authorized payments and reduced budget expenditure without any coherent plan. 'This led to the slow decay of public education, health care, infrastructure, law and order institutions, fundamental research and development, etc.... There were numerous cases of government failure which further undermined the credibility of the state.'[128] Despite expenditure cuts, the deficit of the budget in the first half of 1994 exceeded 8 per cent of GDP and it grew over 10 per cent in the third quarter. This was financed partly by government bonds and partly by direct central bank finance and arrears, including wage arrears, as foreign money was not available. In addition, the government issued its own money, called 'promissory notes' of 50 to 300 day maturity, which were paid in lieu of cash to enterprises supplying the state. Recipients could use these to settle their own debts to other enterprises to reduce inter-enterprise arrears and they were to be accepted in payment of tax liabilities.[129]

Inter-enterprise arrears

The size of inter-enterprise arrears was particularly troublesome in 1992, when their amount was estimated to fluctuate between 20 and 40 per cent of GDP, and in 1994, when arrears reached 10 per cent of GDP. The reasons for the sudden increase of inter-enterprise arrears were mainly economic including the tightening of credits and the quasi absence of credits to enterprises from commercial banks. The allegation by neo-liberal experts that 'the ultimate problem of inter-enterprise arrears is low morale' is not sustainable in the light of the facts, which clearly indicate the interrelationship between the followed credit policy and the size of the arrears and, furthermore, detracts attention from the lack of appropriate institutions and the mistakes made in economic policy.[130] Of course, in this rudimentary Russian economic environment, the business community did react to the lack of appropriate rules and institutions and specific entrepreneurial cultures were developed. As it was observed 'managers often close their eyes to bad debts of their partners due to bribes or special favours that were received in the past or may be received in the future'.[131] In the circumstances characterized by tight credit policies, economic units simply failed to pay for delivered goods and services, thereby creating substitutes for trade credit with no nominal interest rates. A particular feature of 1994 was that arrears were composed of a much higher proportion of wage and tax arrears than before and were concentrated much more in the energy sector or on payments for energy.

The practice of arrears had a lot to do with weak legal rules and institutions in the area of debt collection and with the fact that most Russian enterprises did not face hard budget constraints. The Russian bankruptcy legislation, which entered into force only in 1993, was ineffective. The Federal Bankruptcy Agency, which came into operation by mid-1994, declared about 1400 enterprises insolvent by the beginning of 1995, but only a few hundred of them were put into liquidation.[132] The ineffectiveness of the related judicial system was also a problem, which made debt collection difficult.

The exchange rate and Black Tuesday

The nominal exchange rate of the rouble against convertible currencies depreciated by about 200 per cent in 1993. In real terms, it depreciated until early 1993 and appreciated substantially in the rest of 1993 and at the beginning of 1994. The Central Bank begun to intervene in defence of this trend from mid-1994. As the fiscal and monetary situation deteriorated, this intervention became increasingly massive. But reserves of the CBR were too low to allow intervention for a long period. On 11 October 1994 (Black Tuesday), in the absence of any central bank intervention, the rouble depreciated by about 20 per cent against the US$ which caused panic and controversy over possible conspiracy and profiteering concerning the crash of the domestic currency. The positive aspect of Black Tuesday was that it clearly demonstrated that 'financial markets can and will abruptly penalize unsound credit policies.'[133]

Privatization in Russia

The establishment of a market economy in Russia needed the privatization of the economic units in order to create a real market. But it

was also a political objective for two main reasons. First, privatization, if correctly implemented, could enhance the popularity of the
reform process as a whole. Second, privatization could deprive
branch ministries of the power they had over Russian industry. The
privatization programme, adopted in the middle of 1992 and its
implementation suggested that economic objectives were largely
overruled by politics. The programme was inspired by the Czechoslovak model, as the liberals who were in charge of the undertaking
considered the Hungarian privatization strategy, which was based
mainly on sales, 'not very successful' and slow. The Polish example
was also rejected for similar reasons.[134] Some had other views.
G. Yavlinsky and B. Fedorov wanted to sell enterprises to the highest
bidders.[135]

Russian privatizers were led by A.B. Chubais, one of the main
liberal-minded reformers, who was appointed minister of privatization and chairman of the State Committee for the Management of
State Property (GKI) in November 1991. Chubais was instrumental in
the establishment of a reform-minded GKI administration, the working out of the privatization programme and its quick implementation. He was close to the President, which certainly facilitated the
promotion of privatization. This explains why, after the adoption of
the programme, when the relationship between Parliament and the
executive power became extremely tense, conceptual decisions relating to privatization took the form of presidential decrees, frequently
reversing legislative acts of the Supreme Soviet.

According to the privatization programme (which included all
state and municipal property except for state farms, land and housing) assets in state property had to be transferred into private hands
within only 18 months, which indicates that the speed of the process
was considered a decisive element. Under the programme, workers
and managers were given the right to shares in state property under
preferential conditions, sometimes practically free of charge. Local
authorities were charged with implementating of the privatization
process and were entitled to a major part of the privatization proceeds. Branch ministries received special treatment only in some so-
called 'strategic' sectors. The programme covered three enterprise
categories: small enterprises, which were already transferred to municipalities in 1991, which were to be sold through competitive bidding
or lease buy-out; large enterprises, which first had to be converted

into open joint-stock companies whose shares, after corporatization, were to be sold or distributed depending on the procedure followed; and medium-size enterprises which were free to choose either the direct sale or the corporatization method. Real estate was excluded from the initial privatization programme, which was one of the reasons why most privatized entepises did not own the land and the buildings they occupied. Local governments preferred to lease commercial real estate on preferential terms than to sell it. This situation created ambiguities between user and ownership rights and left the future of these rights uncertain.

Mass privatization, which was implemented through the use of vouchers distributed to all citizens, was mandatory for 5000 large enterprises and optional for about 20000 medium sized enter-prises.[136] Privatization plans were to be submitted by the enterprises themselves in which one of the three privatization options, approved by two thirds of the work collective, had to be indicated.[137] Option 1 was chosen by 25 per cent of enterprises, while 73 per cent chose Option 2 and, only 2 per cent were in favour of Option 3. Enterprise assets were sold in three stages: first, a closed subscription for employ-ees to buy shares under the conditions of the option chosen and second, the sale of a certain amounts of shares in public voucher actions, and third, the sale of remaining shares against cash at public auctions.

In terms of statistical data, the results of Russian privatization are outstanding. By September 1994, 100 000 enterprises had been pri-vatized and more than 80 per cent of the industrial workforce was engaged by privatized enterprises. By June 1994, over 75 per cent of small scale business was privatized.[138] As assets were given virtually free to employees, it was of no surprise that in medium sized and large companies managers and workers became owners of an estimated 65 per cent of the shares. Of that, about 8.6 per cent on average belonged to top managers. The ownership of the rest of the shares was divided between outsiders (21.5 per cent) and the government (13 per cent).[139] Foreigners owned less than two per cent of the stock. Between 1994 and 1996, ownership by employees went down to 58 per cent of the stock, the share of outsiders increased to 32 per cent and the state owned 9 per cent, while the proportion of employee-owned firms fell from 90 to 65 per cent.[140] There are reports, however, that the number of enterprises dominated by management was much larger than indicated by the data, and management was quite hostile to outside investors and employees who resigned were likely to be put under pressure to sell their shares to them.[141]

After the end of the voucher based privatization in mid-1994, authorities started to organize sales of remaining shares in the form of auctions. However, 'cash privatization was more sluggish than anticipated in 1995 and 1996'.[142] Under the 1995–96 'loan for shares' programme, banks competed to offer loans to the government in exchange for blocks of shares of large state-owned companies. The shares served as collateral, if the government failed to pay back the loans, which was taken for granted, the banks could keep the shares. Banks were expected to compete with each other in tenders with the idea that the bank which offered the best conditions, won the tender. Due to irregularities and corruption the programme was very controversial.[143] The banks which organized the tenders did their best to prevent competition, exclude foreigners and 'only the naive were shocked to find that the only bidder was the bank that had won the right to conduct the auction.'[144] Under the programme, blocks of shares of the best Russian companies were obtained at low prices by a small number of privileged banks and individuals, or in other words, by the 'new Russians'.

The privatization programme for 1998 included the privatization of 70 companies. However, the collapse of the equity market, continued devaluation fears and other problems undermined these plans. As a result, most privatization programmes, including the privatization of shares in large companies like Lukoil (oil), Gazprom (gas) or Svyazinvest (telecommunication) had to be postponed or put on hold. Attempts to privatize Rosneft (oil) also failed in 1998.

Privatization in Russia has resulted in a very high level of insider or employee control in companies. As workers and management are convinced that new shareholders could jeopardise their position, they are hostile to outside investors, especially foreigners. This, together with other circumstances (such as the denial of ownership of the company regarding the land they occupy or the costly social services delivered by companies to their employees) have made investments in privatized enterprises unattractive. As a consequence, not much structural adjustment has taken place since privatization. The present owners do not have the capital for the needed investments, new investors are not welcome for the reasons mentioned, and the banking system is neither willing nor capable of financing restructuring. The weakness and unpredictability of the Russian legal and institutional system has added greatly to the plight of the new enterprises. The lack of appropriate legal regulations also favoured excessive control by company insiders as minority shareholders were not protected against their abuses. The underdeveloped capital markets, lack of financial information and appropriate ownership registration also facilitated these abuses.[145] Newly privatized enterprises were run by managers as workers were badly organized and had no influence on the board of directors. Outside shareholders, even if they had a significant block of shares, were unlikely to be represented on the board and the insiders virtually always elected the general director.[146]

This situation has not really been changed by the adoption of new laws and regulations on cumulative voting or other questions. In January 1996, a new corporate law entered into force, which reflected the requirements of a market economy in general, but in practice it has not significantly influenced enterprise behaviour. The corporate governance remained 'horrible' and insiders continued to dominate privatized companies and the inefficiency of the judicial system has facilitated the survival of the old practice.

Privatization of land has not yet been finished. About 62 per cent of land is privately owned, but the majority of it was in the form of collective ownership. The remaining 38 per cent are still owned by the state or local municipalities. In 1997, private farmers cultivated 3 per cent of total agricultural land. In 1998, new laws on land registration and mortgages were enacted, but the adoption of a market oriented Land Code was again delayed, which remains a major obstacle to property markets being developed.

Deepening of the crises despite some improvements on the surface (1995–98)

In Russia, in sharp contrast with Central and Eastern Europe where average economic growth was already at the levels of 5.6 per cent and 4 per cent in 1995 and 1996, aggregate output continued to drop by 4.2 and 6 per cent respectively, in these two years. Industrial and agricultural production and productivity continued to fall substantially, only small enterprises and joint ventures reported some growth in 1996. Aggregate domestic demand was severely depressed. Real wages, for example, fell by 26 per cent in 1995 and registered unemployment, despite underreporting, exceeded 11 per cent by 1997. The crises in Russian society also deepened. There were, however, some positive changes, such as the process of disinflation, but as we will see later, a very high price was paid for that. In 1997, at last, after seven years of steep economic decline, the Russian economy seemed to come back, as real GDP increased by 0.8 per cent. But the revival was short-lived, economic activity weakened already by the second quarter of 1998 and returned to a steep downturn after the collapse of the stabilization efforts on 17 August 1998.

A new stabilization programme and the illusion of improvements

In early 1995, in collaboration with the IMF, a stabilization programme was prepared whose priority was the reduction of inflation. The programme was characterized by tight monetary policy and was supported by a standby loan of US$6.3 billion released in monthly instalments. At the same time, direct credits from the CBR to cover the budget deficit were discontinued, to be replaced by sales of treasury bills and bonds. After this decision the government bond market saw a very fast development, with the GKOs (treasury bills), OFZs (federal loan bonds) and MinFins (hard currency denominated bonds) as the main instruments. Access for foreigners to the GKO/OFZ market was authorized in early 1996 and was further eased later. The CBR was granted a considerable degree of independence from the government. The target for the deficit of the federal budget was set at 7.8 per cent of GDP for 1995. CBR interest rates were linked to the rates prevailing on the interbank market. In the middle of 1995, a RB/US$4300–4900 fixed exchange rate corridor was introduced. This nominal anchor, combined with high interest rates had a stabilizing impact on economic expectations and led to a very substantial real appreciation of the rouble. For the first half of 1996, a new exchange rate corridor was fixed (RB/US$4500–5150) with the objective of slowing this down.

In February 1996, Russia's new stabilization programme, which was supported by a three year IMF agreement on an Extended Fund Facility (EFF) loan of US$10.1 billion, included the following main targets: substantial reduction of inflation; increasing confidence in the rouble; and lowering the federal budget deficit. The programme continued with tight monetary policy and introduced changes in the exchange rate policy. The fixed peg system was replaced with a crawling band with a pre-announced rate of crawl from mid-1996. The exchange rate evolved within the pre-announced bounds, but at the cost of occasionally significant interventions of the CBR on the foreign exchange market. In the second half of 1996, the real exchange rate depreciated by 5 per cent.[147] The tight monetary policy resulted in very high but strongly fluctuating nominal and real market interest rates between 1995 and 1998. Fluctuations of interest rates were also influenced by political events such as the presidential elections in 1996.

In this period, Russia, despite strong pressures for protectionist policies, maintained a liberal foreign trade policy. Export quotas and licenses were eliminated in early 1995, as were all remaining export duties on strategic goods in June 1996. The system of strategic exporters was also eliminated in 1995, and all enterprises became eligible to engage in export activity. Other administrative export control measures, such as pre-shipment contract registration requirements and mandatory quantity, quality and price certification were abolished in March 1996. The repatriation of foreign exchange proceeds was monitored through the 'passport' system of exchange registration. A similar system was in force for monitoring prepayments for import purposes. Only a few goods, such as weapons, radioactive materials, alcohol, and precious metals and stones were subject to import licensing. There were frequent changes in import tariffs, but the trade weighted average duty rate remained around 15 per cent. Almost all dutiable items remained in the zero to 30 per cent range. Most tariffs were applied on an *ad valorem* basis. In 1995, discretionary import duty exemptions were eliminated, but granting exemptions under Russia's customs law remained a widespread practice. These exemptions included imports of humanitarian aid, contributions to the charter capital of joint ventures and equipment for the mass media. Therefore, duty collection remained much below the average statutory rate. The main instrument of protectionist pressures was the Safeguard Commission, which was considering applications from a number of companies requesting the introduction of import protection measures.

From late November 1997, the negative effects of the Asian crises were also felt in Russia. In defence of the weakening rouble, CBR further raised interest rates and the rate of inflation consequently declined sharply. The rise of the consumer price index, which reached almost 200 per cent in 1995, was at the level of 14.7 per cent in 1997, lower than in the most successful transition economies, namely Hungary or Poland. These changes boosted domestic and foreign confidence in Russian stabilization policies. For 1998, almost all sources projected tangible growth.[148] Foreign investments started to increase, the Russian Stock Exchange experienced an unprecedented boom and it became the best performing stock market in the world in 1997. There was euphoria among Western business people who, together with many Russians, driven by their desire to profit quickly from the Russian boom, totally misinterpreted the nature of the changes and mistook their dreams for reality.[149] They took the sustainability of the economic revival for granted and failed to see that the seemingly positive developments masked the crumbling of the whole structure of the Russian reforms. The IMF, which always based its judgements mainly on macroeconomic developments and programmes, was also optimistic.[150]

The real situation in Russia

The real social and economic situation in Russia was quite different in 1997 and in the first half of 1998 to the one described in documents prepared by official sources, international organizations and neo-liberal experts, who had been calling Russia a 'market economy' for years. The success of the authorities in reducing inflation, the booming financial markets and increasing foreign investments diverted attention from underlying problems such as the very low quality of the business environment and economic imbalances which were not addressed, or not properly, during the seven years of reforms. In the area of microeconomics, the root of the problem was the lack of real privatization. On paper, enterprises became private, but in reality they did not behave like privately owned entities. In terms of enterprise restructuring, not much happened. Investments fell back, the average age of equipment in industry exceeded 15 years in 1997, the share of equipment aged under 5 years dropped to 8 per cent of total equipment in 1996, while it was around 40 per cent in 1970. Managers and workers, the new 'owners', did not feel the necessity for structural changes, as resources were concentrated on keeping insolvent enterprises alive. This shoddy practice was due to a generally weak legal framework and the social safety net functions of the enterprises, such as accommodation, medical care and kindergarten provision for workers and their families. As the state was not capable of taking over these social functions and insolvent enterprises, for social policy reasons, were not pushed into liquidation. It was no surprise that the percentage of lossmaking enterprises was constantly increasing.[151] Both the workers and the management were interested in maintaining the *status quo*. But even if they had wanted to introduce changes, the lack of a supportive economic background would have prevented them. In these circumstances, classical macroeconomic measures, which could have been successful in other situations, led to perverse consequences.

The monetary policy which followed resulted in an extreme demonetization of the country, with deadly side effects.[152] Austerity measures drove real interest rates very high, prolonging the recession. And high interest rates greatly increased the costs of financing the state budget deficit. At first, only Russians could obtain GKOs, which were sold to finance the deficit, but the liberalization of the government securities market for foreigners from 1996 resulted in a substantial inflow of speculative portfolio capital into Russia. The share of GKOs held by foreigners increased sharply and so did yields on government securities.[153] At the same time, stock exchange prices declined sharply. The rapidly growing public debt absorbed liquidity, which hampered both macroeconomic and microeconomic restructuring. Economic units could not borrow money due to high interest rates, and interest rates remained high as a consequence of continued government borrowing. Investment in GKOs seemed very profitable for the privileged Russian commercial banks which, instead of dealing with problematic domestic clients, borrowed convertible currencies in Western financial markets and bought high-yielding government securities and shares.

The tight monetary policy and the lack of enforcement of contracts contributed to the growth of non-payments. At the end of 1996, the stock of arrears was estimated at almost twice the stock of domestic currency in the economy.[154] Most arrears continued to grow in 1997. By June 1997, total enterprise arrears to suppliers reached 12.5 per cent of GDP (up from 9.4 per cent in June 1996). Total enterprise wage arrears also continued to grow, they amounted to 2.2 per cent of GDP in mid-1997, a 0.7 per cent increase year-on-year. Millions of workers were not paid at all, or only partly, or in non-monetary form, mainly with the products of their enterprises.[155] Enterprise arrears to the banking sector remained at 5.6 per cent of GDP.[156]

Collection of taxes was a constant problem right from the beginning of the transition period. The tax regime was a remainder from Soviet times and was totally inappropriate to the needs of a market economy. It was not the nominal tax burden which made taxation extremely onerous for business but rather its structural characteristics. The tax regime lacked transparency. It was governed by around 2000 legislative acts; the total number of taxes at federal, regional and local levels exceeded 200. Sometimes, taxes were applied retroactively. Different versions of the draft Tax Code were discussed in the Duma, but the text was never approved. Authorities gave many tax exemptions, tax deferrals and other privileges for political considerations. As firms and other taxpayers tried to avoid paying taxes, tax compliance decreased and tax evasion grew.[157] The very strict penalty systems and the establishment of a special tax police did not improve tax collection, but largely contributed to helping the corrupt practices of tax collectors. Problems of tax collection were magnified by tight monetary policies. The demonetization of the economy made tax compliance very difficult even for those enterprises which were willing to pay (a rare exception). The widespread use of barter transactions complicated tax control and led to paying taxes in non-monetary forms or as offsets against public expenditure.[158] As a result, by June 1998, tax arrears increased from 5.8 to 6.4 per cent of GDP within one year.

By early 1998, the share of barter in industrial sales reached a mind-boggling 50 per cent and the use of monetary surrogates such as promissory notes (veksels) also proliferated.[159] The use of barter and veksels helped to avoid the banking system and largely contributed to tax evasion. As one study argued, 'tax avoidance is the primary explanation for the rise of barter and surrogate money in the Russian economy'.[160] Veksels were accepted by regions as tax payments, which also promoted their use. This explains why arrears to the Federal budget were consistently higher than to its regional counterparts.[161]

The low level of domestic public confidence in Russian reforms and the future of the country in general were indicated by the massive capital flight right from the beginning of the reform process. This was particularly clearly revealed in 1996 and 1997, when inflation declined sharply and the rouble was considered a stable currency. The perversity of the situation was that Russian capital, which knew perfectly well that Russia was in a deep crisis, deserted the country while foreign investment increased as foreign investors gave credence to optimistic macroeconomic forcasts. Between 1992 and 1997, the amount of capital flight was estimated to be in the range of US$127–158 billion which constituted a continued and very serious drain of financial resources. The amount was close to the total net external debt of the country.[162] The reasons behind this massive capital flight, beyond the general distrust in Russia's future, were many, but they certainly included political uncertainty, bureaucratic obstacles to investing in Russia, unfavourable tax treatment, the possible return of high inflation, the neglect of property rights, the lack of adequate corporate governance and the problematic ownership structure of most Russian firms.[163] The collapse of the rouble in August 1998, has further increased the outflow of capital. Administrative controls on preventing capital flight have not been properly implemented.

In light of these absurdities, it is not surprising that Russian enterprises behave differently than economic entities in a normal market economy environment. In the fight between the formal and informal rules, the latter won. Enterprises reacted accordingly. Barter, tax avoidance, alliance with the criminal world, lossmaking and postponement or avoidance of restructuring, became the rule. In 1994, only 31 per cent of enterprise directors mentioned profit as one of their top two objectives. In 1995, this share declined to 27 per cent and in 1996 to 21 per cent.[164] During the years of economic transition, just as happened in the Soviet economy, a virtual economy emerged. 'The virtual economy has arisen for two fundamental reasons: most of the Russian economy, especially its manufacturing sector, takes away value, and most participants in the economy pretend that it does not. Barter, tax arrears, and other nonmonetary methods of payment turn out to be the main mechanism used to sustain the pretence. The pretence is what causes all the non-payment difficulties. There is less value produced than there are claims on it.'[165] In other words, the crises of the Russian economy is much deeper than it appears from official GDP figures.

In the legal and institutional fields, developments were also contradictory. In the Duma, a large number of draft laws were introduced in the 1994–95 session and later. The successful legislative activities covered such important economic issues as the Civil Code (1995–96), laws on the Central Bank (1995), natural monopolies (1995), joint companies and limited liability companies (1996) and insolvency (1998). But, as the struggle between the executive and legislative branches continued, the Duma failed to adopt the draft Tax Code and the Land Code. The introduction of operational systems for mortgage and pledge and registration on legal entities were also left pending.

Despite some positive developments the legislative situation remained rather confused. Institutions, which were necessary for the smooth functioning of a federalist system, were not in place. Legal rules and decisions taken at federal level often contradicted measures introduced at the levels of the 89 subjects of the Constitution, or locally. The different types of federal legal acts were often contradictory, due to the conceptual differences between the Presidency and the Parliament.[166] A special problem, inherited from the Soviet system was, the lack of legislative traditions and legal experts with legislative experience. There was a 'tendency to write very general laws and decrees. Individual cases are then dealt with in very specific ministerial regulations or by decrees and orders dealing with the particular case, leading to a plethora of incoherent decisions.'[167] The weakness in the law manifested itself in vague, contradictory and inconsistent formulations, isolated law-making divorced from international legislation, conflict between laws which had been centralized and the republics, between the republics themselves, between the republics and their autonomous territories, and the instability of unclear laws which change from day to day.'[168]

A particular feature of the Russian situation in the area of laws and institutions is that legal rules, however perfect they may appear on paper, are generally not, or not properly, enforced. The reasons behind this are partly historic, as mechanisms of contract enforcement and voluntary law-abiding behaviour were always weak in Russia. The divided nature of the Russian court system, which was inherited from the Soviet period, is also a contributory factor to non-satisfactory contract enforcement. The arbitration courts hear legal disputes between business entities. Ordinary civil courts have jurisdiction over cases between individuals. The constitutional court is a new forum with the task of reviewing constitutionality of legislation and the resolution of disputes between the federal institutions and the regions. As it was noted, the problem is that 'there are three systems that might hear similar disputes, the rate of development of precedents and predictability of the law will be retarded.'[169] But even in those cases where judicial decisions exist, there are serious problems with enforcement as voluntary law-abiding behaviour is rare and the state has not provided the institutions and rules which are necessary for enforcement of court ruling. However, as many business people confirm, the main difficulties in doing business in Russia 'are due more to uncertainty about government actions than contractual weaknesses.'[170] Russian administration works slowly, it is unpredictable and frequently corrupt. A comparative study indicated that 'it takes, on average, four times as long to set up a new business in Russia as in Poland, and that such businesses are subject to significantly more inspections and other cumbersome regulations.'[171] There are many examples of Western companies having avoided the Russian market or having slowed down their investments because of the weak legal system, the intrusive, unpredictable and corrupt nature of the administration and the court system. These weaknesses are to a very large extent responsible for the low level of foreign investments in Russia.[172]

The sharp increase of corruption and organized crime is probably the darkest side of the transition process. However, this is not to suggest that corruption did not exist in Russia in earlier times. In Tsarist Russia, officials were paid little and they were generally considered to be pervasively corrupt at all levels. Later in Soviet times, corruption was also widespread, but it took different less monetary forms, as cash, convertible currency and quality goods were in short supply. The size and depth of corruption, however, was strongly limited by the very strict control over all aspects of life exercised by the party and state apparatus. Of course, it is very difficult to compare the level of corruption before and after the introduction of major reforms. The result of a 1994 opinion poll indicated, however, that 47 per cent of the sample felt that 'bribery was more prevalent today' than during the Brezhnev period; '34 per cent believed that the respective levels were about the same, and only 4 per cent felt that Breznev-era bureaucrats were more susceptible to bribery than their present counterparts.'[173] All available information suggests that after the collapse of the totalitarian Soviet regime, Russia has become one of the most corrupt countries in the world. According to the index published by

'Transparency International', which ranked 52 countries, Russia was the 49th most corrupt country in 1997.[174] The Economic Intelligence Unit Risk Service which covered 97 countries, gave Russia and four other CIS countries the highest rating for corruption among public officials. The DRI McGraw-Hill Global Risk Service gave 12 CIS countries the average corruption score of 64 per cent, a level only slightly exceeded by the countries of sub-Saharan Africa.[175]

In Russia there are over one million bureaucrats who have been given, by laws and regulations, probably with the intention to create an environment susceptible to corruption, wide discretionary powers. This situation, together with the fact that wages and salaries in the public sector are at such a low level that it implies that officials, following old Russian traditions, are going to be 'fed by clients'. During the last few years of the reform process, substantial wage arrears being the rule rather than the exception in the public sector, has provided an extra incentive for corruption.[176] According to estimates, at least 70 per cent of all officials are corrupt. Commercial companies allocate from 30 to 50 per cent of their profits to bribe authorities. Some suggest that each official has his price. Expensive officials include those working in the banking and finance spheres, who have the powers to provide loans on concessional terms. According to the data provided by the Ministry of Interior, up to 40 per cent of a loan returns as cash to the pocket of the issuer. An especially dangerous development of the past few years is the growth of corruption among 'the political and even ruling élite'. This is a direct threat to the weak Russian democracy. Corruption is of special concern in the areas of law enforcement, customs and tax, and supervisory agencies. The quick mass privatization, as we saw earlier, has contributed to the criminalization of the economy.[177]

Corruption and organized crime support and feed each other. The extent of criminality and total disrespect for law has reached such dimensions that public perceptions concerning some basic elements of social relations have changed. According to an August 1997 poll, 52 per cent of the respondents to the question 'who do you believe runs Russia?', selected: 'the mafia, organized crime' as their reply. Only 21 per cent chose: 'state authorities'.[178]This public feeling precisely corresponds to the conclusions drawn by a recent study prepared by the Russian Academy of Science's Institute of Sociology which states: 'organized crime and corrupt government officials control over 40 per cent of the Russian economy, including approximately two-thirds of all commercial institutions, 35 000 businesses, 400 banks, as many as 47 stock exchanges, and 1500 government-owned enterprises.' It was also revealed that 35 to 80 per cent of the shares in different financial institutions were controlled by Russian criminal organizations.[179] Most commercial undertakings have to pay 'protection money', ranging between 10 to 50 per cent of turnover to stay in business.

Crime and corruption has affected practically all segments of social, economic and private life. Public security has worsened dramatically, reflected especially in a very high homicide rate.[180] Even the payment of salaries is influenced by crime as, according to first deputy prime minister A. Chubais's estimation, embezzlement and financial manipulation by managers accounts for 'at least 50 per cent' of wage arrears nationally.[181] Tax evasion has become a national sport for both individuals and business entities. Copyrights, trademarks and other intellectual property rights are generally ignored. The International Intellectual Property Alliance estimated that 'nearly 100 per cent of videos sold in Russia are pirated and the Software Publishers Association estimates that the rate of piracy of computer software in Russia is 95 per cent.'[182] The whole society can be characterized by pervasive lawlessness and universal disrespect for legal institutions including courts and other legal procedures, 'regarding them as corrupt and arbitrary'.[183] As a result, 'Today a citizen, an entrepreneur, is compelled to equally protect himself against the violation of his rights both by criminal elements and by the state apparatus.'[184]

In summer 1999 reports revealed that Russian organized crime used a New York bank for laundering about US$10 billion. Experts expressed concern that 'Russian criminality reaches the highest levels of government – is, indeed, often indistinguishable from it.' The fear was also voiced that the evil of organized crime, woven into Russian life, 'is starting to infect the rest of the world.'[185]

The Russian state does not fulfil its basic function in contract enforcement or in providing protection against criminals for individuals and business. What the state can not do, the mafia can, or at least makes an attempt to carry out. As a result, the mafia is heavily engaged in both contract enforcement and protection of business, demanding a high price for its services and forcing people to pay with threats of physical harm or murder.[186] Of course, the observation that 'there are reasons to doubt that the Mafia will actually provide an efficient level of contract enforcement' is quite correct.[187] As President Yeltsin declared, the 'criminal world has openly challenged the state and launched into an open competition with it.'[188]The state's lack of action reinforces the feeling in business that tax evasion is the right thing to do as 'they are having to pay separately for services the state should provide.'[189] As the state does not fulfil its functions in the social sphere either, it is not surprising to find that the mafia also plays a role there. 'Membership of a gang can provide an identity, a place in a hierarchy, in a time of anomie and chaos. More importantly, they can offer security, not just for the moment, but also for old age...at a time when state pensions are almost worthless. In short, the Russian mafia is often seen not so much as a parasite but rather as vital.'[190]

The role of regions

After seven decades of strong Soviet centralization, when frictions between vastly different regions and Moscow were suppressed by force, the period of reforms has brought decentralization into the relationship between the centre and the provinces. The 1993 Constitution defines Russia as a federation of 21 autonomous republics and one autonomous region, six territories (krays), forty-nine oblasts, ten autonomous districts (okrugs), and metropolitan centres (Moscow and St Petersburg). These 89 'federation subjects' form the intermediate level of government. Local governments (at county, city and village levels) are subordinated to the administration of these federation subjects. Differences between regions in terms of economic development, languages, religion or traditions are enormous. Controversies with independence-minded Muslim regions have taken the form of open wars, as demonstrated by the examples of Chechnya and Dagestan.

According to Article 71 of the Constitution, the exclusive jurisdiction of the Russian Federation includes the determination of the basic principles of federal policy and federal programmes in the fields of economy, environment and the social, cultural and national development of the Federation; establishment of the legal framework for a single market; financial, monetary, credit and customs regulation, emission of money and guidelines for price policy; federal economic services, including federal banks; the federal budget; federal taxes; standards; development and control of energy, transportation, communications and space programmes and policies. The joint jurisdiction of the Federation and the subjects of the Federation include international relations of federation subjects, tax administration, ownership and use of land and natural resources, and the selection of court and law enforcement officials. Article 74 provides that 'No customs frontiers, duties, levies, or any other barriers for free movement of goods, services, or financial means may be established on the territory of the Russian Federation.'

The relations between the federal government and the provincial governments are vaguely defined and not transparent. They are governed by bilateral arrangements which provide for different degrees of autonomy in different areas. 'Some provinces managed to bargain successfully for special rights even after the adoption of the new constitution of the Federation; *e.g.* the 1994 treaty between the federal government and the republic of Tatarstan permits the latter to have its own constitution, tax system, foreign policy and foreign trade policy.'[191] The concern over the capability of federal institutions to maintain a unified legal system seems to be perfectly justified.[192]

Between 1992 and 1994, more than 70 presidential decrees and resolutions of the federal government granted special rights and powers to 14 autonomous republics and the three oblasts.[193] The degree of autonomy of different republics also depends on their constitutions. In 1992, Chechnya declared itself a sovereign state. This declaration led to a large-scale military intervention of the federal authorities. Events in Dagestan and in Chechnya again in 1999 have demonstrated that separatism will be a long-lasting problem in Russia.

Local administrations introduced all kind of restrictions in their territory, often in clear violation of federal or even constitutional laws. They restricted exports of specific goods and imposed restrictions on some activities (for example banking). The city of Moscow and some oblasts imposed restrictions on free residence. In 1996 and 1998, the Constitutional Court invalidated the statutes of a number of regions which held these restrictions to be inconsistent with the Constitution. The restrictive illegal practices, however, have been maintained.[194] After the economic collapse of 17 August 1998, price controls were introduced on basic foodstuffs (in Krasnoyarsk), and a state of emergency was declared (in Kaliningrad), again in violation of relevant federal laws.[195]

From the point of view of economic reforms, two basic types of economic region can be distinguished: 'extrovert', which include resource-rich provinces and major commercial centres, and 'introvert', which include provinces dominated by military–industrial complexes or agro-industrial provinces. Extrovert regions generally support liberal economic reforms and trade policy and favour Russia's integration into the world economy. The populous agro-industrial regions favour protectionist policies to keep food prices low through, mainly illegal, price and export controls; a popular approach as it shields inhabitants from economic shocks. Regions dominated by heavy and armament industry follow different policies. Some are reform-minded, hoping to attract foreign investments, while others try to secure more state subsidies.[196]

As centralization has been loosened, the gap between regional wealth and poverty has widened. The resource-rich provinces and Moscow are wealthy; the rest are poor. Revenue sharing between the regions has become a politically sensitive and difficult task. In 1992, provincial governments received the right to keep a certain percentage of taxes collected under their jurisdiction.[197] However, the whole system remained opaque and became a constant fight between the central government and the provinces. In 1994, major changes were introduced into the system, but 'on the whole, discretion continues to play a major role in the budgetary process.'[198] Between 1995 and 1997, further progress was made in the area of fiscal relations between different levels of government, but 'the rules, agreements, and laws themselves remain highly unstable, excessively complicated, and often contradictory.'[199] Later, the Primakov government exerted substantial pressure on the regions to alter the distribution of consolidated budget revenues in favour of the federal authorities. The fight over the distribution of revenues between the centre and the provinces is far from being over.

The collapse of the Russian economy on 17 August 1998

In 1997 the Russian economy experienced a small recovery which raised false expectations both inside and outside Russia. The deteriorating external economic environment, however, soon brought the unsustainable state of affairs in the Russian economy and society to the surface. As a result of the Asian crises, the prices of primary commodities, accounting for about 80 per cent of Russia's exports, fell sharply leading to a major deterioration in the country's external and fiscal balances. Conditions in international financial markets became unpredictable and volatile making the financing of the increasing Russian fiscal imbalance more expensive. The tightening of fiscal and monetary policies led to high interest rates, which squeezed the economy further. In the second quarter of 1998, economic decline resumed. As no hard budget constraints were imposed and budget revenues were stagnating or declining, the increasing budget deficit had to be financed from external sources which created a heavy and increasingly deleterious burden on the economy. Relations between the government and the IMF became tense and, as a consequence, at the beginning of 1998, the IMF suspended its financing of the deficit under the three-year Extended Fund Facility.

The increased borrowing requirements of the budget forced the government to raise the yield on short-term treasury bills (GKOs), which remained the only source of deficit financing, to make them attractive for investors. The rouble came under considerable pressure as foreign investors started leaving the Russian GKO market when they realized the risk associated with the fact that foreigners were holding about US$25 billion of roubles in GKOs while CBR reserves had decreased to the level of US$14.5 billion.[200] Russia's new government, headed by S. Kiriyenko, was forced to increase drastically GKO yields in order to lure investors to alleviate the pressure on the rouble and to make money available for meeting government obligations, including the payoff or rollover of previous loans. (The appointment of Kiriyenko, who replaced the summarily dismissed V. Chernomyrdin, was approved by the Duma after a month long tug-of-war with the President, at the end April 1998). On 27 May, the CBR, in a quasi noninflationary environment, tripled its refinancing rate to the crisis level of 150 per cent. Russian high officials, including the Prime Minister and the President, repeatedly said that no devaluation of the Russian currency would take place. Temporarily, the pressure on the rouble subsided, especially after the IMF resumed funding under the Extended Fund Facility and indicated, as did US officials, that a new financial assistance package might be offered dependent on a new austerity package being adopted.[201]

The anti-crisis programme was primarily composed of emergency fiscal measures aimed at raising tax revenue and austerity measures aimed at reducing government spending. The lack of political consensus over the programme was manifest when the Duma passed only some of the draft legislation proposed by the government. As time was running out, the executive introduced the most important measures required by the IMF in the form of presidential decrees. At the same time, the President also vetoed certain laws voted by the Duma.[202] In July, a rescue package of US$22.5 billion was put together by financial institutions. Within this package the IMF pledged to lend US$11.2 billion to Russia in 1998, plus 2.6 billion in 1999. The rest of the money was to be raised by extraordinary official loans and additional World Bank lending.[203] But the downward spiral could not be stopped. The first tranche of the new IMF credit, US$4.8 billion, had to be spent in defence of the rouble. Demand for GKOs vanished completely, even though yields on short-term bonds were raised to 300 per cent. The outflow of capital continued until the government could no longer meet service payments due on domestic debts and defend the rouble at the same time.

On 17 August 1998, the government and the CBR announced emergency measures which marked the beginning of a new and very deep crisis in Russian political and economic life. The measures announced 'effectively amounted to floating the rouble, a 90-day moratorium on the servicing of (private) foreign debt by local commercial entities, and mandatory restructuring of part of the rouble denominated domestic debt.'[204] After the introduction of these measures, financial markets became chaotic. The rouble started its free fall and by the end of 1998 it had lost about 70 per cent of its value. Administrative foreign exchange control measures were introduced. The Russian stock market also collapsed, together with the banking system. The depreciation of the rouble reduced imports and inflation started to pick up. At the end of the year the consumer price index reached 80 per cent. Decrease in output accelerated; GDP declined by more than 5 per cent by the end of 1998, exports and imports contracted by 16 and 18 per cent, respectively.[205] Around 40 per cent of the population lived below the poverty level. Tax collection suffered another blow.

In early 1999, Russia started its slow economic recovery. During April–June, industrial output exceeded the levels of one year earlier by about 5 per cent. This trend was continued throughout the whole year. According to the IMF, 'The recovery appears to have been primarily led by import substitution following the depreciation of the rouble.'[206] Monthly inflation slowed down to under 2 per cent in June and the budget deficit also fell. Following the recovery of energy prices and a sharp compression of imports,'[207] the external current account, on cash basis, swung from a deficit of US$2.7 billion in the first quarter of 1998 to a surplus of US$4.8 billion in the first quarter of 1999.[208] Russia's 1999–2000 economic programme, which assumes a rescheduling of nearly all obligations on Soviet-area debt due in this period, focuses on fiscal adjustment and the acceleration of structural reforms. Inflation is expected to decline to 50 per cent by the end of 1999, while forecasts on the contraction of GDP is 2 per cent. According to the Programme, the government remains committed to a liberalized trade regime and has promised the abolition of foreign trade restrictions introduced after the August crisis. It will continue negotiations toward WTO accession and any new trade restrictions would be fully consistent with WTO rules.[209]

On 28 July1999, the IMF approved a 17–month stand-by credit for Russia of US$4.5 billion to support the government's 1999–2000 economic programme. The credit will be disbursed in seven equal parts, with the first instalment released immediately. About the nature of the Russian economic crises, the IMF Executive Board declared that 'the economic crises that erupted in 1998 had been due mainly to the failure of the authorities to come to grips with longstanding fiscal problems and to implement structural reform. The deterioration of the external environment as a result of the Asia's economic crisis had been only the immediate cause of the crises in Russia.'[210]

4
What Went Wrong With Russia's Economic Reforms?

After more than eight years of political and economic reforms, Russia is still in serious trouble. The cumulative decline of GDP has exceeded 45 per cent, while poverty among the population is widespread, and unemployment is substantial and constantly growing. The Russian state can not fulfil its functions and crime and corruption have developed international dimensions. The spectacular collapse of the Russian economy on 17 August 1998 revealed the crisis to be deep and comprehensive. Since that date, the government of Russia, supported by international organizations, has tried to work out a new programme which could correct the mistakes which led to the disaster. It is obvious that the future of Russia's economic transition is of utmost importance for the country's accession to the WTO. A country without functioning trade-related institutions is in no position to assume its obligations in the organization. Here an attempt is made to identify the major mistakes committed at the beginning of the reform process and to identify the root causes of Russia's economic decline. Without such an analysis no remedies can be offered for the resolution of the problems. The conclusion of the chapter is that the major mistakes made by reformers include the total misunderstanding of the importance of historical traditions in Russia's economic reforms; the preference given to shock therapy methods; violation of democratic principles; and neglecting institutional aspects of reforms.

Initial conditions of reforms and the role of historical traditions

The first big mistake made by Russian neo-liberal reformers, their foreign advisers and certain international organizations was that they overlooked Russia's unique history and assumed that the country's economic transition process would follow textbook recommendations applied by other countries. They chose Poland's shock therapy transition from centrally planned economy to market economy as the most relevant model.[211] It was true that Poland, like Russia, at the beginning of the transition process, had serious macroeconomic disequilibria characterized, among other things, by high inflation and budget deficit. But otherwise the differences between the two countries, rather than the similarities, were striking.

And the major difference was that Poland, a country dominated by catholicism, belonged to the West rather than to the East. Before the Second World War, Poland had a functioning market economy. Soviet-type socialism was imposed on Poland only after 1945 and was always thought of by the majority of the population as an alien system which disrupted the continuity of Polish history. This public feeling showed itself in uprisings and demonstrations in 1956, 1968, 1970 and from 1980 in the establishment and popularity of Solidarity. In Poland, socialism was never applied in its full rigour as in the Soviet Union. Agriculture, which produced about 30 per cent of GDP, remained mainly private. Private property and market relations in other areas were also tolerated to a much greater extent than in the Soviet Union, where all institutions and relations which could be associated with capitalism (bar a few rare exceptions) were prohibited. Poland, unlike its big Eastern neighbour, made several reform attempts during the socialist years. The 1989 Polish shock therapy was preceded by eight years of semi-market reforms. In addition, Poles were never totally isolated from the outside world and prewar market economy institutions could be revived with success. During the years of socialism, Poles were allowed to travel and maintained strong relationships with an influential Polish emigré population in the United States and other Western countries. Polish citizens had a more or less realistic picture of the market economic system and were unified in their wish to support political and economic reform and a 'return to Europe'.

Russia, compared to the Central European former socialist countries, has had distinctly different historical traditions, which have made it more difficult for her to assume Western political, legal, economic and trade institutions. But it was not just seven decades of totalitarian dictatorship and planned economy which made the transition process in Russia much bumpier. For a full understanding of Russia's present problems the relevant chapters of the country's earlier history also have to be studied. The differences between Russian and Western political, legal and economic approaches and institutions are rooted in the differences between Western European and Russian history.

The Western part of Europe inherited a sophisticated legal structure, and the Latin language, from the Roman Empire, while Russia and other territories to the east, did not. After the schism between Rome and Byzantium in the 11th century, Russia became a member of the Eastern orthodox world. Western Europe, including the peoples living in the territories of today's Poland, the Czech Republic, Slovakia, Hungary, some parts of Romania and Yugoslavia, Slovenia, Croatia or the Baltic states, sooner or later also followed Western Christianity and cultivated a sophisticated Roman law based legal culture which later formed the institutional and legal structure of Western capitalism. During these centuries concepts of the rule of law, including the supremacy of law over political authority, emerged as a result of the struggle between different legal systems. 'Whether it was the struggle between the ecclesiastical and secular authorities, or, as in the case of England, the struggle between ecclesiastical, mercantile, common law, and equity legal systems, the countries of Western Europe learned a great deal about principles of defining and limiting jurisdiction, much of it drawn from Roman law.'[212] In Western Europe, the period of the renaissance, reformation, enlightenment and the major revolutions from the 16th century onwards were all centred around the rights and obligations of individuals and institutions. During these centuries, the institutional foundations of capitalism were laid down. Some countries of Central Europe were part of these developments, albeit, less fully than countries to the west.

The concept of the rule of law, however, has been missing from Russian culture and legal traditions. The Orthodox Church, contrary to the Roman church which maintained and cultivated an independent and parallel identity to the state, 'rejected the independence and supremacy of the papacy and remained an integral part of the state. In this way, Russia missed the most important foundations of the western concept of the rule of law.'[213] In this backward, state dominated environment, a special power oriented culture took root. This is one of the main reasons behind Russian society's overwhelming respect of power and strong central institutions and its correspondingly weak tradition of voluntary law abiding behaviour. Russia (and also many other countries which had non-Western Christian traditions such as Turkey, Japan or Egypt) 'adopted Romanistic legal forms – principally legal codes – in the eighteenth, nineteenth, and twentieth centuries.'[214] Orthodoxy provided fertile ground for the development of Russian autocracy. 'Over the centuries, in medieval Muscovy, the Russian Empire, and the Soviet Union, the autocratic government required personal service from most if not all its subjects, issued a host of arbitrary laws, and remained immune from constitutional restraints on its executive power.'[215] This peculiar Russian legal background makes it understandable why the reform of Russian law 'to accommodate the emerging capitalist economy conflicted with the desire to maintain autocratic rule.' And why conflicts were resolved 'in favour of autocracy'.[216]

After the Bolshevik Revolution, the poorly developed market-related institutions were quickly destroyed and a centrally planned economy was introduced.[217] In Russia, where socialism was considered 'home grown', a fundamentalist approach dominated in both politics and economics. Resistance to the communist take-over or attempts to reform the new system was brutally suppressed. Law was subordinated to party politics and ideology. The country, throughout 75 years, remained totally isolated from the West. In light of her difficult pre-1917 history and the destruction of three generations of Soviet power, it would have been difficult to find a country worse suited to a 'big bang' type market economy transformation than Russia. All suggestions that at the beginning of the reform process the situation in Poland (or in any of the countries in central and eastern Europe which shared historical roots with the West) and in Russia were similar, are totally unfounded. Later events have proved, unfortunately, that the 'homo sovieticus' not only existed, but its cross-breeding with Russian history has conspired to create a market alien environment which will be difficult to eliminate. The therapy that was concocted from the idea that Russia had similar initial conditions to other former socialist countries could not have been anything but wrong.[218]

Despite the unfavourable historical backgrounds, a fatalistic approach regarding Russia's economic future is not suggested. For market-oriented reforms to succeed strategies, policies and methods should be developed which take account of historical deficiencies. Russia is a country of outstanding talent and its great contribution to arts and science is beyond doubt. But it is also true that 'since the time of Peter the Great certain of its social institutions (the army and its associated system of defence, schools, science and art) have had a "Western" appearance, while other spheres of life – especially those associated with work, everyday life, and people's leisure time – are clearly "Eastern".'[219]

Reforms must not be exhausted in drafting perfect, text-book laws. All reform measures must be accompanied by a clear concept of implementation. Substantive decisions need to be preceded by thorough analysis on the feasibility of implementation. The existence of institutions, which are indispensable for implementation, should not be taken for granted in Russia. Adoption of laws which can not be implemented further degrades the legal environment, leads the country further away from the rule of law and plays into the hands of the mafia.

The general improvement of the whole institutional and business environment in Russia needs a comprehensive strategy and a lot of time and patience. If the country wishes to become a modern market economy, basic behavioural patterns of the nation should be changed. This unprecedented historical 'reprogramming', however, needs modesty and stamina. The shortage of knowledge due to history has to be ameliorated through education. Every citizen of the country need to learn at all levels of education and otherwise, how states based on rule of law and market economies function. And how individuals find their place in such a new environment. Fears are not justified that Russia would lose its identity and be westernized if it undergoes such a process. The motivations behind human behaviour are deeply engraved in human minds over long histories and can not be changed substantially overnight. Better to say only history can change such a sophisticated pattern of motivations. But this historical correction process has already started in Russia. The question now is how can this new challenge be met in the least painful way and within the shortest possible time. The outlook is good. Russia has one of the most educated populations in the world and its people have demonstrated extraordinary qualities and discipline when the fate of the country was at stake. If Russia learns how to excel in spheres of life which are 'associated with work', it has the potential to become an economically successful country. Unfortunately, we can already see what will happen if Russia does not adequately meet the market economy challenge. The trend that has been started may continue and the country may become a place without functioning institutions, populated by poor people, dominated by mafias and oligarchs, with an underdeveloped, isolated economy engaged mainly in the production of raw materials and energy for exports. Or, the other available alternative, it may become a dictatorship again, with the already well known consequences for its own population and for the outside world.

Gradualism or shock therapy?

The second tragic mistake made by Russian reformers was their religious devotion to a big bang approach, even though in Gorbachev's Soviet Union there was a 'nearly universal belief in the necessity of gradualism in the transition to a market economy.'[220] Neo-liberal economists, especially the Russian government's foreign advisers, however, urged a comprehensive 'big bang', stating that 'gradual transition from a planned to a market economy is impossible.'[221] Or, as expressed in other words, 'It does seem that the worst place to be is in-between capitalism and communism, and the best policy is to hasten through that phase as rapidly as possible.'[222] They referred to prior experiences of stabilization and systemic changes elsewhere, notably in Poland, and to the dominant current economic theory, which, according to this interpretation, suggested that 'a swift and comprehensive change, comprising as many simultaneous measures as possible, is most likely to minimize the social cost of transitions.'[223]

Neo-liberals praised Poland and Czechoslovakia which had introduced versions of shock therapy and criticised Hungary for its gradualist approach. But Poland[224] was also subject to negative comments because its shock therapy, unlike in Russia or Czechoslovakia, did not include rapid privatization. It is worthwhile to quote Åslund's devastating words about the dangers of gradualism in respect to privatization: 'Hungary and Poland, on the contrary, have been left with a large number of unprofitable and parasitical state enterprises that demand massive subsidies and thus pose a threat to both stabilization and welfare. The surprise is that the Russian government did not make more serious mistakes in such a quick process.'[225]

Another critical comment, which again amply indicates that neo-liberals have misunderstood the significance of historical legacies and the decisive role of institutional development in economic transition, was: 'contrary to widespread belief, the Hungarian economic reforms have, on the whole, placed the country in a less advantageous position than the more orthodox policies of Czechoslovakia, and that, as a result, the Czechs have in fact enjoyed … an "advantage of backwardness"'.[226] One wonders why foreign investors have not shared this view and for what reasons the gradualist Hungary has been, by far, the number one country in terms of per capita foreign investments, and why this country, according to most institutions, has become the leading or, at least, one of the leading transition economies.[227] The answer is evident. Hungary had already started its economic reforms, or, one could now say, its economic transition from central planning to a market economy, in the 1960s. Decades of gradual developments, with their ups and downs, strengthened the country's market institutions which resulted in Hungary's substantial 'reform advantage' over other countries in the region.

Contrary to neo-liberal statements, successful transitions in history have mostly been gradual, especially in democratic societies, where shock therapy policies have been the exception. This follows from the sophisticated interaction which exists between economic reform policies and the related political, legal and other institutions. Postwar Western European reconstruction and the history of GATT, provide excellent examples supporting gradual changes and not for drastic ones. Despite all convincing textbook type theoretical arguments for quick liberalization, trade in textile and clothing will be brought back under GATT disciplines only after more than four decades of deviation during a 10-years-long transitional period. Trade liberalization in agriculture has only started during the Uruguay Round but will be on the agenda of future rounds of trade negotiations. Many contracting parties, including developed ones, had maintained quantitative restrictions on imports of many industrial items in conflict with basic GATT rules for decades. The substantial decrease of customs duties has required about five decades and there are still many high tariff peaks even in developed countries.[228] The main arguments against quick liberalization were, and still are, that a speedy elimination of restrictions would impose an unbearable burden on the sectors and whole regions concerned. And what about Russia? Should not we apply the same standards?

In democratic countries it would be very difficult to introduce radical changes without some form of social consensus and the existence of a social safety net which could provide some compensation for those who became net losers due to the new policies. But the establishment of a broad social consensus needs a sophisticated political and civil society infrastructure in which all major interests groups are represented through political parties, employers and workers organizations. In Western democratic societies this framework has been shaped in decades, or centuries, by long debates in parliamentary and other fora. No democratically elected government can afford to alienate itself from substantial segments of society through the sudden introduction of new policies without offering appropriate compensation to those whose interests have been negatively affected by the changes. All interests should be taken care of, including those that do not represent the 'right cause'.[229] But of course, the identification of the interests concerned, their confrontation, finding appropriate solutions, compensation and adjustment is time-consuming. But time invested in finding social consensus is rewarded by social stability and the ensuing capacity for continuous development. All these considerations are valid for Russia and should have been applied.

Attention was already called to the dangers of ultra-radical reforms in the early 1990s. Russia and the other countries that introduced these reforms were warned that the degree of social support lent to reforms would depend on the presence of social safety nets. This would determine the extent of the shock that could be endured by the population without derailing the reform programme. It was also pointed out that the argument 'that trade and price liberalization cannot be introduced gradually is simply not true.'[230] The point was also made that 'rapid price and trade liberalization may be destabilizing in a transition economy with inelastic supply responses, which are partly due to institutional rigidities, and with inadequate

instruments and institutions for creating and maintaining macroeconomic stability.'[231] However, all these considerations were swept
aside. As a result, Russia has a disastrous economic situation, institutional chaos and public opinion hostile to reforms.[232]

Introduction of shock therapy in a Bolshevik way, facilitated by the weakness of Russian democracy

The third mistake (if mistake is adequate) made by the reformers was
the Bolshevik way of introducing shock therapy. Neo-liberal Russian
reformers quickly realized that after the general social fatigue that
followed the ideological and economic chaos caused by Gorbachev's
half-reforms and the August 1991 conservative *coup d'état*, the conditions for an immediate introduction of the shock therapy were
excellent. They took advantage of the fact that new pressure groups
and political structures did not exist, or were very weak, and that old
pressure groups were demoralized.[233] It is not difficult to recognize
the anti-democratic, putsch like nature of the neo-liberal 'revolution'
which was imposed on the Russian society, a truth which was
admitted by some protagonists: 'Politically, it is easier to have a big
package of radical measures accepted early on, when a deep sense of
crisis prevails and various interest groups cannot yet fully evaluate
what they may gain or lose.'[234] Neo-liberals complained that 'Even
reasonably knowledgeable Soviet reformers have great difficulty
understanding what a market economy actually entails.'[235] Of
course, the rest of the population, the 'man in the street', knew
even less about market economy and were totally ignorant of what
the immediate consequences of the radical reforms would be. The
only thing that people knew for certain was that they did not want to
live as before. But it was also clear that the civilizational, human and
institutional preconditions necessary for a radical market economy
reform were not present.

Taking advantage of the population's overwhelming wish to have
a better life and the popularity of the President, the neo-liberal
'vanguard', representing a fraction of the population, exploited the
power vacuum. They took the leadership and in the form of presidential decrees, without any constitutional or political base, or social
consensus on the nature and depth of the changes, imposed an ill-
conceived, untested reform policy on Russia, ignoring the country's

historical background and current possibilities. Again, a revolution from above in Russia. It was rightly noted that the manner of its introduction was 'more reminiscent of the *coup d'état* of 1917 than the democratic revolutions of 1989.'[236]

Shock therapists, arguing for radical reforms, frequently manipulated public opinion with the spectre of the return of the 'old guard' and caricatured the proponents of gradualism as conservatives. During the Soviet decades millions died in the gulags and practically all Russian citizens suffered. It was ironic, therefore, when Russian citizens, who still vividly remembered the years of dictatorship, were lectured about the dangers of communism by young reformers and foreign advisers. In the August 1991 *coup d'état*, the 1993 referendum and the 1996 presidential elections, Russians clearly expressed their strong views that they supported changes and did not wish to return to Soviet methods. But parliamentary elections also clearly indicated that radical reforms were not accepted without reservations.

Russia has paid a high price for the authoritarian introduction of its reforms with ensuing clashes between an executive with wide powers and the parliament. The presidency still represents (though frequently inconsistently) reforms, and the parliament the gradualist Russian majority. The fights between these two institutions have simply been the expression of the society's reservations about the radical reforms imposed on the country. This original mistake is the root cause behind the failure to achieve a consensus over the future of Russian reforms, thus preventing efficient solutions to Russia's major economic problems being found. Reformists may be right in saying that many members of the Russian Duma can be characterized as conservatives. But it must be remembered that these conservatives have been sent to parliament by popular vote, making out-of-hand rejection of their position by the executive, questionable.[237] Russia can not and must not have a more progressive parliament than it can form through democratic elections.

Russian democracy is far from perfect. It was called by one author 'imitation democracy', suggesting that it is based on the import and assimilation of Western political institutions, similar to democracies in other countires, like in Japan or Latin America. Therefore, one could rightly say that Russian democracy 'is at the beginning of a long road. Imported mechanisms are operating, but still constitute a formal framework, a shell, the wrapper of an oligarchic, corporatist regime with extensive links to criminal sectors . . . . It may take several election cycles, perhaps even generations, before Russia develops a civil society that will articulate its interests and channel them into the political sphere, thus filling the existing mechanisms with real democratic contents.'[238] It is this deficiency in democracy which is the main cause behind the underdeveloped and chaotic nature of Russia's economic institutions.

Lack of market economy institutions

The fourth mistake of Russian reformers was the introduction of radical market reforms without the existence of the necessary supporting institutions and the misunderstanding of the role of the state. Nothing that has been said above suggests that an economic shock therapy can not be successful. 'Big bang' approaches may be successful when radical policies are supported by a decisive majority of the population and the necessary institutional background for sudden changes is present, or can be established or re-vitalized within a short period of time. This was the case in Hungary, Poland, the Czech Republic and even in some of the former Soviet republics, namely in the Baltic countries which had different, more market friendly historical traditions than the rest of the Soviet Union.

In Russia, however, radical economic reform policies and stabilization measures have failed to produce the expected results. Liberalization, deregulation and privatization have not created a stimulating economic environment as they did in most countries of Central and Eastern Europe and the Baltic states. After nearly a decade of economic reforms one can draw the conclusion, that without appropriate political, legal and economic institutions, even right policies will fail. In Russia, reform and stabilization policies, which may have been right in different circumstances, could not be implemented because these policies, for the historical reasons detailed above, were alien to both the population and the existing institutions. In addition, shock therapists neglected the building of institutions, and concentrated on macroeconomic policy measures instead. They were also convinced that the existence of state administration was the source of corruption. Their ultimate conclusion was that Russia 'should adopt much more liberal conditions than usually exist in the West.'[239]

The direct cause of the Russian crises was a major fiscal imbalance. However, the economic collapse in August 1998 was just the expression of a deep economic and political crisis. The problems, at the beginning of the transition process, were started by a more than 40 per cent decline in GDP between 1989 and 1996, accompanied by very high inflation. The 1995 stabilization programme, supported by the IMF, was based on tight monetary control and strict exchange rate regulation. The Central Bank stopped the direct financing of the deficit budget, which was instead financed through state securities. These measures promoted price and exchange rate stability in 1997 and in the first half of 1998. But Russia paid a very high price for this 'stabilization'. Not only were the stabilization measures tailored to the needs of a functioning market economy, but in their interaction with the existing institutional vacuum, they have accelerated the perverse reaction of business and society to the radical reform measures introduced. In addition, the provisional 'success'[240] of stabilization made Russian reformers and international organizations over optimistic, and strengthened their conviction that right macroeconomic policy, rather than building institutions, was the key to further success. They did not seem to realize that the weakness of state and social institutions distorted reforms and facilitated the rapid rise of criminality and mafia rule.

Privatization, which was implemented with revolutionary zeal, has produced enterprises that are formally private but do not behave as private entities. The main reason behind that is the absence of regulatory, financial, banking and other institutions which are necessary for their normal functioning. Tight monetary policies led to demonetization of the economy that facilitated or even enforced the widespread use of barter and tax avoidance. More than half of existing industrial capacity was destroyed, while active adjustment of enterprises to the new market situation was very slight, or almost non-existent. Banks were fragile and invested mainly in GKOs instead of lending to domestic enterprises. Decreasing budgetary income coupled with the anti-state approach of reformers further weakened state administration and contributed to the disintegration of social infrastructure and the widening of differences between rich and poor. Parallel with the imperfect functioning of society, in the institutional no-man's land, crime and corruption has flourished. Thousands of new laws and regulations were adopted, but have proved to be rootless. For historical reasons, law-abiding behaviour was an exception rather than the rule. These factors, together with the weak judicial and administrative system have prevented the consistent implementation of new laws. In such an environment the level of foreign investment was low and a huge amount of domestic capital left the country. A contrary development would have been a miracle.

As a result of the 'weak state' concept, state intervention into the economy was kept to a minimum and industrial policy rejected as a matter of principle, overlooking the fact that the governments of the transition economies were being forced into adopting industrial policies *de facto*.[241] In general, the positive effects of trade liberalization are beyond doubt. In Russia, however, these positive effects could not manifest themselves because the adjustment capabilities of the economy were very limited. These interrelated elements resulted in the creation of a pseudo market where the Russian economy could not but become virtual. The 'institutional hiatus' was a major reason for the general chaos and unexpected severity of the slump in output in Russia (and in some other transition economies).[242] Since the collapse on 17 August 1998, it has generally been recognized that the absence of necessary institutional reforms was responsible for the failure of Russia's stabilization efforts.[243]

Regional problems

Russia's sophisticated federal structure adds a special dimension to the country's political and economic problems. The Federation encompasses areas that have greatly differing religious and other, including business, traditions to the Russian parts of the Federation. There is a serious danger that the armed conflicts with the Muslim regions, Chechnya and Dagestan, are just the first two acts of a much longer drama. Another problem is that the new federal structure of Russia has not been working efficiently. The constant struggle between the centre power and the regions has prevented the implementation of federal laws. The other side of the coin is that regions may take measures which conflict with Russia's international obligations. The weakness of implementation is a constant problem between the centre and the regions.

5
The Road to WTO Membership

Basic rules on WTO accession

The GATT was not a formal international organization and therefore it had contracting parties and not members. Given that the WTO has been established as an international organization, states or separate customs territories may become its members in accordance with the rules contained in Articles XI and XII of the Marrakech Agreement Establishing the World Trade Organization (WTO Agreement). Of course, accession to the WTO is more complex than it was to the GATT, requiring the acceptance of the WTO Agreement and all the multilateral agreements which extend the scope of obligations beyond trade in goods to such new areas as trade in services, trade-related aspects of intellectual property rights, a more stringent dispute settlement system and the trade policy review mechanism.[244] Accession, however, does not require the acceptance of the plurilateral trade agreements (Agreements on Trade in Civil Aircraft and Government Procurement), which are included in Annex 4 of the WTO Agreement.[245] As a result of the Uruguay Round, the WTO has become a global organization which administers trade institutions in the areas mentioned above.

The WTO Agreement makes a distinction between original and new members. The contracting parties to the GATT 1947, who accepted the WTO Agreement and the multilateral trade agreements and for whom schedules of concessions and commitments were annexed to the GATT 1994 and schedules of specific commitments were annexed to the General Agreement on Trade in Services (GATS), became original members of the WTO. For others, Article XII provides the possibility for accession on terms to be agreed between the applicant and the WTO. In respect of substantive rights and obligations, however, there are no differences between original and new members, as according to Article XVI:4 of the WTO Agreement 'Each member shall ensure the conformity of its laws, regulations and administrative procedures with its obligations as provided in the annexed Agreements.' It is interesting to note that the WTO Agreement does not define any procedural rules to be followed in accession itself. The individual Working Parties which provide a framework for accession negotiations have substantial freedom to shape their own procedures. However, in practice, they all follow the traditions applied by the GATT 1947 under its Article XXXIII.

The WTO accession is a unilateral procedure because it is the acceding country which has to conform to the rules of the WTO system; the rules of the WTO are not negotiable in the accession process. The acceding country during the accession negotiations has no right to request additional benefits from members. The subject of accession negotiations is twofold: (a) to determine how and when the acceding country will comply with the rules of the WTO; (b) to determine the 'membership fee' which will be paid by the acceding country in tariff concessions and commitments, including commitments on trade in services, in exchange for the benefits of trade liberalization achieved in previous multilateral trade negotiations. Decisions on accession are taken by a two-third majority of the members of the WTO.

What are the main general considerations behind WTO membership ?

While the GATT 1947 was established by 23 countries, the Marrakesh Declaration, which marked the conclusion of the Uruguay Round, was signed by 124 governments plus the European Community. By the middle of 1999, the number of WTO members reached 134, representing more than 90 per cent of world trade. In August 1999, there were 32 applicants and one can state that almost all major trading countries are already members or have made steps to gain membership in this organization. After the accession of all the current applicants, which include China and Russia, the WTO will truly become really a universal trade organization.

Motivations behind joining the WTO may vary from country to country but there are some basic issues more or less common between all accession-related decisions made by governments. Certainly, all countries, independent of whether they are developed, developing or transition economies, would like to have better access for their exports of goods and services to the markets of WTO members. The countries which do join the WTO enjoy all the trade advantages which the multilateral trade system offers, such as lower tariffs and reduced non-tariff barriers which were negotiated in the framework of eight previous multilateral rounds with all the necessary legal guarantees, including the settlement of disputes. That in itself makes WTO accession for all trading nations attractive. But it is also obvious that for countries without major bargaining power such improvements in market access are normally not achievable bilaterally. If countries with small bargaining power do manage to conclude bilateral trade agreements which quantitatively seem to provide, due to the inclusion of m.f.n. provision, the same treatment in the area of tariff and non-tariff measures, the legal stability and the enforceability of these arrangements remain questionable. In addition, bilateralism does not promise further improvements in market access which WTO principles and mechanisms do. Therefore, quantitative and systemic benefits provided by the multilateral WTO system largely exceed the advantages any bilateral arrangements can offer.

Beyond these general considerations, accession of countries in transition to the WTO, under appropriate terms, may contribute to the success of the transition process through the strengthening of their domestic policies and institutions and by the introduction of greater stability and predictability in their trade policies.[246] WTO membership can help governments in their fight against anti-reform forces, quickly strengthening protectionist pressures and the traditional isolationism which was so wide-spread in most former socialist countries. International institutions in general, but the WTO system in particular, can provide necessary guidance and may constitute an 'external anchor' in the transformation process of domestic trade institutions and in the formation of economic and trade policies. WTO membership can also help in the elimination of the discriminatory trade barriers which were introduced by some WTO members in the cold war period against some of the countries in transition, as they are likely to violate the non-discrimination principle of the

WTO. Transition economies are also aware that WTO membership encourages foreign investment, as it guarantees a greater predictability and transparency of trade-related institutions.

The WTO is considered, rightly, as a vehicle of globalization which contributes greatly to the unification of the basic rules of international trade. If the rules of the game are the same or similar everywhere and are enforceable world-wide, advantages associated with globalization will become more accessible to all participants in the system. Therefore, there is a common interest to make the membership of the WTO universal.

Considerations behind Russia's WTO application

It is certainly of great interest to recall what were the major considerations behind Russia's application for accession at the beginning of the process, and to determine how these considerations have changed in the light of developments in the accession negotiations and the country's economic reforms.

Considerations by Russia

When the Russian representative announced in the GATT Council in June 1993 that Russia had decided to apply for accession to the GATT, he focused mainly on Russian reforms and qualified the application as a logical constituent part of Russia's economic reform policy. He mentioned only briefly that accession to the GATT would improve trading opportunities both for Russia and its trading partners.[247] Later, at the very beginning of the accession process, in June 1995, at the first meeting of the Russian Accession Working Party in June 1995, the head of the Russian delegation, deputy prime minister O.D. Davydov, put much more emphasis on Russia's expectations of improved market access for its exports. In a clear allusion to the large number of anti-dumping investigations against Russian exporters, he first mentioned 'An end to discrimination on the part of Western countries that do not now recognize Russia's free market economy' as among the important advantages Russia could gain from joining the WTO. Other advantages mentioned included the access to the WTO system of maintaining discipline in international trade; the opportunity to put trade and economic relations 'on an equal, sound, long-term economic and legal basis'; the harmonization of

Russian laws and practices with international requirements and the creation of a 'legal space' which is familiar to foreign companies. He even implied that Russia's final decision about joining the WTO would depend on the extent of improvements in market access for Russian exports.[248]

There is no doubt that, beyond economic advantages, the political aspects of WTO membership have always played an important role for Russia, even if these considerations were not emphasized openly. The disadvantages of non-membership would be especially painful for Russia as, even though a permanent member of the UN Security Council and a super power of the recent past, it would be excluded from the possibility of shaping the international trading environment. It can, therefore, be taken for granted that in Russia's final decision, political considerations will occupy an important place.

At the start of the accession process most Russian statements attempted to prove that as a result of reforms, the country's foreign trade system was already more or less compatible with WTO requirements. Subsequently, as the accession process has unfolded, this line of argument has been mixed with the firm representation of Russian trade interests. In the years after the introduction of economic reforms, the share of energy and raw materials in Russian exports grew sharply, while production and exports of industrial goods decreased dramatically. Because of this, politicians formulated the requirement of strengthening the country's industrial base and integrating Russia into the world economy as an industrialized country.[249] Anti-dumping procedures which treated Russia as a 'non-market economy' were condemned with increased vehemence. In this context, Prime Minister Chernomyrdin pointed out that 'by the level of discrimination we rank second after China. Direct damage alone is estimated 1.7 billion US dollars.... Russia's membership in the World Trade Organization will make sense if the international trade regime for the country becomes better compared to what it is now. Our obligation to open up our markets will be subject to such improvement.'[250] According to another Russian source, by the end of 1995, 41 anti-dumping cases were filed against Russian exporters. Of these cases, the Russian government contended that 22 were unjustified and considered them indicative of overt discrimination.[251]

After several meetings of the accession Working Party, Russian officials started to make comments on the country's general accession conditions. They cautioned WTO members that accession to the organization remained a high priority but Russia would not accept any conditions.[252] In December 1996, at the ministerial conference in Singapore, the Russian representative openly criticized the accession process by expressing the hope that Russia's negotiating partners would refrain from requesting that Russia, or other acceding countries be burdened with 'overly excessive and unjustified commitments, as compared to the obligations of the existing WTO membership.'[253] As the difficulties of making Russia's trade system compatible with WTO requirements became known, Russian experts, adopting a position similar to that of the agro-industrial lobby which sought protection against increasing import competition, suggested following a more gradualist approach. The point was made that the liberalization to be undertaken by Russia in the accession process should begin at a later stage when Russian production capacities had been restored.[254]

Events of 17 August 1998 shook the confidence in the Russian WTO accession process. It transpired that the country's reforms were built on weak foundations and many of the economic liberalization measures were not sustainable. It became clear that practically all the basic elements of the reform package had to be revised. In October 1998, the Russian trade minister visited Geneva and stressed that accession to the WTO remained a priority of the Russian government. He reassured the members of the Russian Working Party that Russia would continue to gradually liberalize its foreign trade regime and that it did not intend to resort to protectionist measures. He also urged Working Party members to continue tariff negotiations with Russia on the basis of the Russian tariff offer.[255] Earlier chapters of this book show that Russia's crisis was comprehensive and that no easy or quick solutions can be offered. The new Primakov government, in office from early September 1998 until May 1999, (similarly to later Russian governments) failed to offer a detailed, new and transparent correction package, but its first stabilization measures included a number of WTO-accession related elements. For example, a new Russian customs policy was outlined, with a strong emphasis on the development of the 'real economic sector' and the restoration and expansion of production 'on a basis of existent and new capacities'. In addition, the government promised better protection of the domestic market through the use of anti-dumping and countervailing duty measures.

Exporters would be subjected to stricter financial disciplines to prevent massive capital flight.[256] It was also obvious that Russia had to strengthen the regulating role of the state in the economy. As the Prime Minister stated: 'Market elements alone cannot resolve anything. Regulation and intervention is needed.'[257] The idea of providing more protection to domestic producers was also reflected in the President's annual state-of-the nation address to the Federal Assembly on 30 March 1999.[258] In order to gain an IMF stand-by credit, the Russian government adopted an economic programme for 1999–2000 in July 1999. According to the programme, the government remains committed to a liberalized trade regime and has promised to accelerate Russia's integration into the global economy and continue negotiations toward WTO accession.[259]

Despite the obvious problems, the Russian accession Working Party continued its work and held its ninth meeting in December 1998 and the Russian delegation was engaged in bilateral market access negotiations with 14 countries. However, since the August 1998 crises, no more self-confident Russian statements have been made on the imminent termination of the WTO accession process. Russian politicians and experts recognized that the road to Russia's accession would be long and bumpy.

Accession of Russia as seen by WTO members

Governments of major trading countries, in full consensus with their business communities, welcomed Russia's and other transition economies' applications for membership to the WTO. Accessions would contribute to the establishment of a truly global, world-wide market where the basic rules of the game would be unified. It goes without saying that the wish to integrate the potentially very large Russian market into the global economy was an especially important consideration for Western governments and businesses. While in the period of East-West confrontation, (as reviewed in Chapter 1) decisions on GATT accessions were heavily loaded by political considerations, approaches to WTO accession issues since the beginning of the 1990s, have become motivated more and more by business interests. Of course, the case of Russia has remained special, because of the size and strategic importance of the country make its integration into the world trading system a world political issue. It is enough to refer to the bilateral nuclear disarmament negotiations between the US and Russia, or to the Kosovo crisis, to recognize that co-operation with Russia in wide political areas is in the interests of international peace and security. Political considerations have not disappeared totally from accession negotiations in the case of some other countries either. For example, politics plays an important part in dealings with countries in which democratic reforms have not been put on the agenda. In the WTO accession of these countries, the position of the major WTO members continues to be determined by both political and economic considerations.[260]

As far as Russia's accession to the WTO is concerned, the positions of all the major trading countries have been worked out with the involvement of their business communities. The US business community has expressed its support for Russia's accession to the WTO under commercially acceptable terms that should involve substantial trade liberalization for goods and services. The fundamental concern of many American businesses was over 'the absence of an effective, enforceable legal system with transparent and uniform laws'. It was at the request of the US business community that this issue, and many other specified problems, be addressed during the accession process with the objective of better aligning Russia with the practices of other markets.[261] The European Commission also found that Russia's legal and institutional framework was weak and lacked transparency, thereby putting a brake on economic recovery. The Commission listed the main areas, such as services, protection of intellectual property rights, standards, certification and border measures, where further liberalization or improvements were needed.[262]

The first major review of accession to the WTO took place at the Singapore Ministerial meeting in December 1996. The new business-oriented approach outlined above was clearly reflected in statements made by ministers and in the text of the Ministerial Declaration which stated that acceding countries should contribute to completing the accession process 'by accepting the WTO rules and by offering meaningful market access commitments.'[263] In May 1998, the relevant language of the second Ministerial Declaration became even stricter by recalling that 'accession to the WTO requires full respect of WTO rules and disciplines as well as meaningful market access commitments on the part of acceding candidates.'[264]

In December 1998, and several times during 1999, the General Council put an item called 'State of play in accession working parties' on its agenda, which involved, in the light of the seven accession negotiations accomplished, a review of some of the major aspects of accessions in general.[265] It is worth recalling the basic positions expressed by different delegations because they are extremely relevant to Russia's accession.[266] A number of developing country delegations recalled that in the accession process unreasonable conditions were required of, and imposed on, applicants because developed country members had requested that acceding countries accept more stringent conditions and a higher level of commitment than was required from members themselves ('WTO-plus' requirement). Reference was made to the mandated adherence to certain plurilateral agreements as prior condition for accession which was not required by the WTO Agreement. Full transparency and objectivity was demanded in accession proceedings. The point was also made that market access commitments undertaken by acceding countries should correspond to the commitments of WTO members at similar levels of development. The view was also expressed that acceding developing countries should benefit from transitional periods if that possibility was provided in various WTO agreements.

Developed country members stressed that new members should comply with WTO rules and commit to an appropriate degree of trade liberalization. Most of them agreed that it was unacceptable to request acceding countries to undertake obligations that went beyond the requirements of WTO Agreements. Regarding the admissibility of transition arrangements, the positions of members differed substantially. A number of developed members were not opposed, in principle, to granting developing countries in special cases transitional periods, while some were basically against such arrangements. According to their arguments, the automatic granting of transition periods was not included in WTO Agreements. The transition periods which were provided for in the Uruguay Round Agreements served a different purpose: they were intended to allow negotiating countries time to become accustomed to the new rules and take steps to adjust to them. Acceding countries were in a different position, they had time to adapt their rules to the WTO requirements during the long transition process. In the case of the six countries which had joined the WTO by the middle of 1999, only a few transition periods have been granted, and were in limited areas and for short periods. By the middle of 1999, it was evident that out of the 32 ongoing accession cases a large number would not be finished by the end of 1999, when the WTO ministerial conference in Seattle was supposed to launch a new round of trade negotiations. For many acceding countries, including Russia, it is an important question as to how and to what extent non-members will be allowed to participate in the new round and how accession matters will be handled during the round. Participation in the new round would provide an opportunity for Russia to express its views both on the agenda of the negotiations and the substantive issues.

It is fair to state that both Russia and its WTO partners have substantially underestimated the time needed for the completion of the accession process. At the beginning, Russian negotiators and politicians thought that accession negotiations would take just a few years. In June 1996, Russia's deputy prime minister declared that 'Russia has already covered half the way toward joining the World Trade Organization, and the year 1997 may become decisive on this road.'[267] At the March 1997 US–Russia summit, the 'Presidents set as a target that both sides would undertake best efforts for Russia, on commercial conditions generally applicable to newly acceding members, to join the World Trade Organization in 1998, and to join the Paris Club in 1997 assuming agreement on conditions of membership.'[268] At the same time, EU officials were more cautious, declaring that Russia was moving in the right general direction but was still at an early stage of the process.[269] In 1998, leading US officials showed less optimism, stating that 'Russia has a very, very long way to go' until it becomes member of the WTO.[270]

Following the August 1998 crisis, nobody now ventures to indicate any specific date for Russia's accession. There is a silent agreement that prior to the stabilization of the Russian economy, the country is not in a position to join.

Procedural aspects of accession

The establishment of the WTO has not significantly changed the accession process; the rules applied by the WTO follow the practice of the GATT 1947, of course with the necessary changes stemming from the WTO's enlarged scope of activities. But the number of accessions to the GATT 1947 was much smaller than to the WTO. For example: between 1973 and 1993, only 28 applicants (1.4 per year) joined the GATT, while since the establishment of the WTO in 1995, 39 applications for membership have been registered. In July 1999, the number of applicants was 32, 18 of them transition economies.[271] Because of the large number of requests, the WTO Secretariat has prepared notes that provide detailed description of the procedures to be followed, information required from acceding governments and the expectations of members concerning applicants.[272] Despite some common procedural practices, accession negotiations are all different, they are carried out on a case by case basis, which reflects the specific situations prevailing in each acceding country. As yet, no agreement has been reached on common accession yardsticks or a range of minimum criteria.

The accession procedure starts with a letter from the applicant to the Director General of the WTO which indicates the wish to accede to the WTO under Article XII. The text of this letter is circulated to all members. The General Council routinely decides to establish a Working Party with the appropriate terms of reference to examine the application and to submit to the General Council recommendations that might include a draft protocol of accession. Membership in Working Parties is open to all WTO members. In the case of Russia, the Working Party has more than 50 members, Ambassador W. Rossier of Switzerland was appointed as its Chairman, following consultations with the applicant and members of the Working Party.[273]

The applicant is obliged to prepare a Memorandum on its foreign trade regime in accordance with the outline format prepared by the WTO Secretariat. In the Memorandum the applicant is expected to describe its general economic and trade policy objectives including: monetary and fiscal policies; the foreign exchange and payments system; investment and competition policies; foreign trade in goods and services; and domestic trade in services. In the Memorandum the applicant is obliged to give detailed information on the structure and functioning of its trade-related legislative and administrative decision making, including the division of powers between central and local governments. A list of relevant laws and regulations together with much other required information; data and publications should be annexed to the Memorandum. The Memorandum should also include detailed explanations of the functioning of import and export regulations and internal policies affecting foreign trade in goods, as well as the trade-related aspects of services and intellectual property regimes. It should provide information on the applicant's bilateral and plurilateral trade agreements and eventual customs union and free-trade area agreements.

The preparation of the Memorandum is a complex undertaking which normally requires technical assistance provided by the WTO Secretariat or some individual member countries. It remains, however, the sole responsibility of the applicant. It should be noted that the WTO, like the GATT 1947, is a member-driven organization, meaning that all substantive and major procedural decisions in accession matters are taken by members and not the Secretariat. In matters of technical assistance, however, the role of the Secretariat, depending on the available budgetary resources, is very important. In the case of Russia, the Working Party was established in June 1993; the Memorandum was circulated in March 1994. The importance of the Memorandum is that it provides the basis of the 'Questions and Answers' stage, which might take years. In this stage members of the Working Party ask questions in written form and the applicant replies to them. Both the questions and the replies are circulated as official documents among members of the Working Party. The circulation of the first questions and answers in the Russian case took place in June 1995, immediately followed by the first meeting of the Working Party in July 1995. The Russian 'Questions and Answers' period has continued since then. Between 1995 and 1997, 3500 questions were raised with respect to the Memorandum.[274]

Once the Working Party considers that it has received sufficient clarification of the applicant's trade regime, the accession procedure enters the phase in which schedules on concessions and commitments on goods and specific commitments on services are negotiated. The fact-finding work on the foreign trade regime and the negotiating phase can overlap and proceed in parallel. The initial schedule of offers in the case of goods, to be submitted by the applicant, consists of proposed tariffs to be imposed and the level at which tariffs are to be bound. (Bound tariff rates can not normally be raised above the levels the WTO member has committed itself.) In the case of services, the applicant tables its draft schedule of specific commitments under the GATS. These schedules identify the extent to which service exporters have guaranteed access to the markets of the member concerned. The applicant is also expected to make commitments concerning the level of support it wishes to provide to its agriculture relative to a base period, which is usually the three years before accession. Commitments should also cover other aspects of support for trade in agriculture, for example, export subsidies. After the introduction of these offers, bilateral negotiations are carried out between the applicant and each WTO member which expresses interest. The subject of these negotiations concern the tariff level or the degree of openness of the service sector offered by the applicant. Negotiations on agricultural supports and export subsidies take place largely at plurilateral meetings chaired by the applicant.

Russia tabled its initial offer on trade in goods in February 1998, while its initial offer on services was introduced only in October 1999. (Negotiators informally called the offer unsatisfactory in the area of financial services.) Bilateral negotiations with Russia have started with 30 members based on the Russian tariff offer and, at the same time, formal meetings of the Working Party continue to address the many remaining unresolved questions regarding the country's trade regime. In March 2000, Russia introduced a revised offer on market access which may reactivate the negotiating process. The new offer includes significant tariff reductions. (Details of the revised offer are not available for the public.) Following the conclusion of bilateral negotiations, the schedule of concessions and commitments to the GATT 1994 and the schedule of specific commitments to the GATS are prepared and annexed to the draft protocol of accession as an integral part of it. A summary of the discussions is included in the Working Party's report to the General Council together with a draft decision and protocol of accession which is prepared by the Secretariat in close co-operation with the members of the Working Party. Protocols of accession follow a common pattern. They make the acceding government a member of the WTO and bind it to observe the rules of the WTO Agreement as rectified, amended or otherwise modified as of the date that the relevant protocol of accession entered into force. The protocol of accession includes the terms of accession agreed by the applicant and the members of the Working Party. Once the negotiations are finished, the Working Party submits its report, together with the draft decision and protocol of accession to the General Council. Following the adoption of the report of the Working Party and the approval of the draft decision by a two-thirds majority of the WTO members, the protocol of accession enters into force thirty days after acceptance by the applicant.

The rapid increase in applications for WTO membership, mainly from transition economies, has posed a number of problems. First, practically all transition economies suffer from weak institutional capacity in the trade policy area and the WTO Secretariat has only very limited resources to assist applicants in overcoming these difficulties. It was, however, a substantial step forward when the Secretariat established the Accession Division at the beginning of 1995. Prior to this, the GATT had no independent unit to deal with accession issues and no explicit resources were devoted to accession matters. The situation though, is still far from satisfactory. As it was noted, 'The five staff of the WTO Accession Division ... are extremely thinly stretched to service even the procedural needs and paperwork generated by more than twenty five active accession working parties.'[275] WTO members also devote a relatively small amount of resources to helping accelerate the accession of new members. It is striking to note that the speed of accession of transition economies to the IMF and the World Bank is much faster than accession to the WTO. This is explained partly by the fewer issues considered in the context of accessions, but partly by the much more generous budgetary allocations devoted to expediting membership of transition economies in the Bretton Woods institutions. In 1991 the World Bank Board allocated $30 million for technical co-operation activities with the Soviet Union and its republics and an additional $15 million was later allocated for expansion of the operational staff working on these countries from about 20 to 150. [276] It shall also be noted as a matter of concern that WTO accession-related multilateral and bilateral assistance is uncoordinated, and sometimes serves the protection of national interests rather than integration of the given transition economy in the international trade system.[277] Therefore, strengthening the institutional capacities of acceding countries through better co-ordinated and more generously funded technical assistance (as actually proposed and financially supported by a number of WTO members) would be perfectly in line with the legitimate demands of governments and business communities to accelerate the integration of transition economies into the world trading system.

6
Main Issues of the Russian WTO Accession Process

It is not yet known when Russia's accession process to the WTO will be accomplished. But the experience which has been accumulated during the seven completed WTO accession negotiations and the more than four years activity of the Russian Working Party provide enough material to identify the main issues which will probably play a prominent role in Russia's accession. In selecting these issues, special attention has been given to the accession conditions of the newly acceded five transition economies, among which three were republics of the former Soviet Union. These conditions reflect the new objectives of the most influential WTO members. Conditions which they are also expected to largely follow in the Russian case. The examination of the main issues concerning the Russian WTO accession will be centred around the three main pillars of the accession protocols, namely commitments on rules; market access concessions and agricultural commitments; and commitments on services.

Commitment on rules and market access conditions

General economic policies

The ups and downs of Russian economic reforms were described in earlier Chapters. As indicated, after several years of inconsistent shock therapy, economic decline has not yet stopped, the economy has not stabilized. Also as described, the reasons behind the economic problems are deep and go far beyond the economy. At present, Russia is at a crossroads. Since the 17 August 1998 collapse, though some specific measures have been taken, no new comprehensive reform correction package has been adopted. It seems to be obvious that in the context of stabilization, such basic questions as the speed of further reforms, the degree of openness of the Russian economy, the role of the state in the economy, the fight against crime and corruption, and the functioning of the legal and the institutional system should be revisited. Decisions in these areas are directly relevant to the country's accession to the WTO. It can therefore be taken for granted that the Russian accession Working Party will be asking Russia to provide information on what changes in its general economic policy it intends. After accession, Russia, like other transition economies, will be expected to submit periodic reports on developments in its economic reforms.

State ownership and privatization

The WTO, similar to the GATT 1947, does not include any direct requirements in respect of the ownership of economic units engaged in trade. But the 50-year history of the GATT/WTO system proves that fulfilment of WTO obligations presupposes functioning market economies. The participation of the Central and Eastern European socialist countries in the GATT demonstrated that state-owned business entities can not meet the requirement of operating fully according to business considerations. As we saw in the first Chapter, in the cases of Poland or Romania, business transactions conducted by state-owned foreign trade organizations were carried out in accordance with plan targets and not business considerations. Therefore, the conditions of accession to the GATT were shaped accordingly. In Hungary's reformed economy, the behaviour of foreign trade enterprises, owned by the state or by co-operatives, was substantially determined by market signals, but they were also subjected to some degree of direct state and party influence at the expense of business considerations. After decades of half reforms, Hungary, and most other former socialist countries, came to the conclusion that for the creation of an efficient market economy the overwhelming majority of economic units must be privately owned.[278] In the light of this historical evidence one can state that the functioning of the WTO system is not unrelated to the ownership of economic units. Economies comprised of privately owned units are far more likely to provide an environment conducive to the full implementation of WTO rules than economies dominated by state owned enterprises.

Therefore, it is logical that, in the cases of transition economies, some members of accession working parties have systematically raised issues related to privatization. The new transition economy members undertook, sometimes reluctantly, the obligation of regularly reporting to the WTO on developments in their privatization programmes and on other issues related to their economic reforms.[279]

In Russia, a large part of the privatization programme has been finished. In 1998, however, due to increasing economic problems, a number of privatization projects were postponed or put on hold. Privatization of land has been hampered by failure to adopt the Land Code. Undefined property rights, as it was indicated earlier, have also negatively influenced foreign investments. A transparent legislation on land ownership would make a big contribution to the Russian stabilization process. The problems associated with the quick and imperfect voucher privatization have also impact on the formation of foreign trade instruments, as restructuring and the increasingly business oriented attitude of newly privatized economic units will necessarily call for some modification in tariff and non-tariff protective measures.[280] There is no doubt that the Working Party, in the context of the country's general economic policy, will continue examining the implementation of the Russian privatization programme until the very end of the accession process and that Russia, as were other transition economies, will be asked to give regular reports on developments in the area of privatization.

Pricing policies

All transition economies and developing countries that have recently joined the WTO maintain administrative price control measures on certain goods and services. Their protocols of accession provide for the publication of any changes in price controls. In addition, they include the obligation that all price controls should be applied in a WTO-consistent fashion and that account be taken of the interests of exporting WTO members as set out in Article III: 9 of the GATT 1994.[281] In Russia the prices of the overwhelming majority of industrial and consumer items are not under administrative price controls. As some goods and services are still subjected to price controls by federal and local authorities, it can be expected that the Russian accession protocol will also include some similar commitments.[282]

Framework for making and enforcing policies

Since the beginning of its reforms, Russia, based on its 1993 Constitution, has established a new political and legal system, which, in principle, could provide a suitable framework for a functioning market economy. State power in the Russian Federation is exercised on the basis of the separation of the executive, legislative and the judiciary. The strong executive power of the president is a special feature of the Russian constitutional system, which has played a very important role in the whole reform period. Experience has proved that in Russia there is an especially large gap between laws and real life. Problems lie mainly not with the texts of adopted Russian laws and regulations but rather with their implementation, which is further complicated by the size of the country and its sophisticated federal system. As the weakness of the legal and infrastructural framework is rooted in the country's history, no quick solutions can be offered.

The accession of transition economies to the WTO and the meetings of the Russian Working Party have revealed which are the sensitive issues in Russia's legal and institutional framework in terms of the Russian accession process. A prominent issue among them is the relationship between the federal and sub-federal authorities.

Authority of sub-central governments

According to Article XXIV:12 of the GATT 1994, it is the obligation of each contracting party to 'take such reasonable measures as may be available to it to ensure observance of the provisions of this Agreement by the regional and local governments and authorities within their territories.[283] A similar obligation is included in Article I:3(a) of the GATS.

In accession negotiations the authority of sub-central governments, if they exist, is always subject to thorough examination by members, because through their actions the integrity of the WTO system might be put in danger. During the accession negotiations with the Kyrgyz Republic, which is divided into seven regional executive administrations, it was confirmed by the acceding country representative that central authorities would be solely responsible for establishing foreign trade policy and that the central government would implement the provisions of the WTO relevant to sub-central governments. The representative of the country further confirmed that, from the date of its accession, the central government would eliminate or nullify measures taken by sub-central authorities that were in conflict with the WTO Agreement when those measures were brought to its attention.[284] Latvia and Estonia have also undertaken similar commitments.[285]

The sophisticated administrative and territorial structure of the Russian Federation and its imperfect functioning has been an issue in the Russian WTO transition process as foreign business people often complain about 'inconsistencies between federal and local regulations, permissions and other requirements affecting imports and investments.'[286] One of the special features of the Russian constitutional system is that the power to regulate foreign trade belongs to the federal authorities, but in issues of direct relevance to the interests of a particular region, federal and regional authorities have a shared responsibility, and regional authorities also play an important role in the implementation of trade-related international agreements. They are responsible, for example, for preventing intellectual property rights violations on their territory. In the area of standards, certification is a further example of joint responsibility between federal and local authorities. While standards are adopted at federal level, local authorities, on the basis of local certification requirements, issue certain certificates.

Members of the Working Party raised the issue that in trade matters they had no clear indication of the precise division of powers between the federal authorities and the republics, and expressed concern over the question whether regional authorities could block the implementation of decisions taken legally at the federal level.[287] The formal answer to this is that, according to the Constitution, federal laws have supremacy throughout the entire territory of the Russian Federation and that the legal mechanism to seek redress against any illegal actions by local authorities is available, as the Constitutional Court has the power to decide whether sub-federal legislation is consistent with federal laws or not. However, as was indicated before, compliance with decisions of the Constitutional Court leaves much to be desired.

Article 74:1 of the Russian Constitution provides that no customs frontiers, duties, levies or any other barriers for free movement of goods, services, or financial means may be established on the territory of the Russian Federation. Obviously, the application of this rule is a basic WTO requirement, but concerns around its implementation are frequent. One of the latest examples was the 'Moscow Alcohol Decree' case. In November 1997, the government of Moscow and the government of the Moscow region issued decree No.792–83 which imposed quality testing requirements and mandatory marking of each product item with a regional bar code. The import and sale of these products had to be carried out only through a single Moscow wholesale retail enterprise. The Anti-Monopoly Committee of the Russian Federation found the decree illegal because it contradicted Russian federal law.

Policies affecting trade in goods (imports)

Trading rights

The protocols of accession of the Kyrgyz Republic, Latvia and Estonia include the commitment to ensure that all their laws and regulations relating to the right to trade in goods, and all fees, charges or taxes levied on such rights, would fully conform with their WTO obligations. Latvia and Estonia, however, maintain specific licensing in the forms of 'certificates of professional qualification' or 'Licence of Activity' on certain entrepreneurial activities which also cover foreign trade activities which are related to the activities subject to authorization.

Foreign trade in the Soviet Union was a state monopoly, exercised by a handful of state-owned foreign trade organizations. The foreign trade monopoly was abolished in 1992, but some restrictions remained in the area of trading rights. Exports of strategically important raw materials were restricted to enterprises registered with the Ministry of Foreign Economic Relations. Only authorized business entities were entitled to participate in centralized import procurement. Export contracts were subject to registration. Enterprises with the participation of foreign capital were authorized to export or import goods of their own production or for their own needs, only if the share of foreign capital exceeded 30 per cent. By 1996, all these restrictions were eliminated. At present, all residents of the Russian federation are automatically entitled to engage in foreign economic activities.[288] In September 1998, the Federal Law 'On Medicines', under Article XX of the GATT 1994, subjected export and import activities in respect of medicines to licensing (licence of activity). The Ministry of Trade issues such licenses.

Ordinary customs duties

The Goods schedule of the acceding country, which forms part of the accession protocol, contains the tariff concessions and the agricultural commitments agreed upon during the bilateral and prulilateral negotiations. Estonia, one of the seven acceding countries which has recently finished accession negotiations, currently does not apply tariffs as it abolished all customs tariffs in June 1998.[289] It has, however, reserved the right, in the form of ceiling tariff bindings,[290] to impose customs duties in the future. All the seven new members bound all items in their tariffs, a move which corresponds to the post Uruguay Round scope of bindings of developed countries.[291] In the agricultural area, for the six newly acceded countries, the simple average of individual tariff bindings ranges between 11.7 (Kyrgyz Republic) and 34.9 per cent (Bulgaria).[292] The simple average of individual tariff bindings on non-agricultural products is between 6.7 per cent (Kyrgyz Republic) and 20.1 per cent (Ecuador).[293] The level of tariff bindings is even lower in Estonia, where most bound rates in the non-agricultural product group are between 0 and 10 per cent.

One can state fairly that the tariff binding commitments undertaken by new members are rather liberal, which expresses the increased requirements of some influential WTO members *vis-à-vis* applicants.[294] Russia uses tariffs as its main trade policy instrument. As indicated earlier, from the beginning of the reform process until July 1992, the application of customs tariffs on imports was suspended. In the first reform years, especially in 1994 and 1995, Russia substantially modified its tariff policy which resulted in considerable increases. In July 1994, import duties were raised across the board, increasing the average weighted tariff from 7–8 per cent to 11 per cent, with some duties reaching 50 per cent. For budgetary reasons, higher tariffs were imposed on goods in most demand, especially food products. In mid 1995, tariffs were rationalized, which led to rates between 5 and 30 per cent on most items. Most tariff peaks were reduced to 30 per cent, except for a number of luxury goods. At the same time, the minimum rate was increased, and most products for which the tariffs were previously zero, became subject to 5 per cent. As a result, the overall level of protection increased to 14 per cent (weighted average). Tariffs over 30 per cent apply to many luxury goods.[295] There were many exemptions granted to institutions to import goods duty free, the implementation of which was far from transparent. These privileges were withdrawn in 1995.

Between November 1997 and June 1998, Russia introduced further adjustments in import duties. These adjustments covered about 2 per cent of tariff lines, two-thirds of the changes represented tariff increases, while one-third tariff reductions, affecting less than one per cent of imports. These adjustments did not result in any change in the weighted average import tariff. In June 1998, Russia decreased tariff peaks from 30 to 20 per cent in respect of 300 items. In July 1998, for balance-of-payments reasons, a 3 per cent import surcharge was introduced on all goods, with effect from 15 August. One of the main consequences of the 17 August 1998 economic collapse was that the rouble depreciated drastically against convertible currencies which led to the sudden fall of imports. Reacting to this new situation, the government exempted basic foodstuffs, medicines and other socially significant items from the 3 per cent import surcharge and reduced import customs duties on a number of food products.

The import of any goods originating in CIS countries is not subject to customs duties in accordance with Russia's free trade agreements with these countries. Developing countries and the least developed countries are exempted from customs duties altogether, while goods coming from developing countries are subject to import duties which are reduced to 75 per cent of the m.f.n. rate.

Exporters often complained about high Russian tariffs, the lack of stability and transparency of the Russian tariff regime, the arbitrary granting of duty exemptions and the complex and frequently confusing customs practices.[296] In response to concerns that the tariff regime was changed too frequently and that tariff rates varied too widely, the government adopted a resolution in October 1997, which stipulated that tariffs could be raised no more frequently than one every six months and by no more than 10 percentage points at a time, with the higher rates taking effect six months after the publication of the changes.[297]

In February 1998, within the framework of its WTO accession process, Russia introduced its offer on market access regarding goods, which included an initial tariff offer. In it, Russia suggested binding its import tariff, in the form of ceiling bindings, on agricultural goods at a significantly higher level than its applied rates. On other goods, too, the proposed ceiling bindings were significantly higher than the currently applied rates in respect of textiles and some other light industry products. Bindings are close to the currently applied rates in a large category of items, which include about 50 per cent of all tariff lines. In respect of products which are considered to be related to the country's national security, no bindings have been offered. In the offer, two levels of bindings are specified. The initial level of bindings would be effective at the beginning of the year following the year of accession. As a main rule, after a seven-year-long implementation period, Russia would apply a lower, final level of bindings. At the beginning of the implementation period, the trade-weighted average of all bound lines would be 24 per cent, to be reduced to 18 per cent by the end of the implementation period. (In respect of agricultural items, the figures are 36 and 26 per cent; for industrial goods: 20 and 15 per cent.)

On the basis of Russia's tariff offer, bilateral negotiations have started between Russia and interested WTO members. Public information about these negotiations is not available, but statements made by officials of some member states expressed dissatisfaction over the Russian offer. The offered tariff bindings were qualified as too high, especially on agricultural products.[298] In reply, Russian officials argued that the low competitiveness of most Russian industries and the requirements of restructuring necessitate import protection, otherwise important sectors, especially agriculture, could be destroyed.[299] As it was emphasized by deputy economics minister I. Matyorov, Russia should take every measure to make the transition period 'as long as possible.... The Russian market can be opened only after the period of complicated economic restructuring is over, stable growth achieved and the budget stabilized'.[300]

A recent World Bank study proposes that Russia, and other transition economies, which are acceding to the WTO, set tariffs at low uniform levels. This strategy 'is likely to be helpful to the longer term development of an internationally competitive and efficient industrial structure as well as facilitate the accession process.' The suggested uniform rate for Russia is 10 per cent, which could be introduced within three years, between 1999 and 2001, through reducing the maximum rates to 10 per cent and raising the low rates to the same level. The study also suggests binding tariff rates at the WTO at rates closer to applied rates.[301] It also warns Russia that 'tariffs are typically ineffective instruments' at addressing the market failure problems of infant industries. Experience has shown that in such cases the 'best intervention is a policy that attacks the problem at the source.'[302]

The level of Russian tariff bindings is one of the key issues in the accession process. Russia and the international community have a genuine problem in finding solutions that are sustainable and serve the interests of both Russia and the other members of the organization. It should be kept in mind that a number of recent historical examples indicate that outward oriented countries with relatively low levels of import protection have developed much faster than those countries which isolated themselves from the outside world through high tariffs and non-tariff barriers. In the case of Russia, a special danger exists if the difference between bound rates and applied rates becomes too significant. It would open the door to protectionist pressure which (due to the lack of an appropriate political, legal and institutional infrastructure representing the interests of different groups and the society as a whole) could result in tariff increases leading to higher than economically justifiable tariff levels. On the other hand, binding tariff rates at very low levels, even at the levels of applied rates, would also be dangerous. Such a situation would not allow any manoeuvring room for the necessary tariff adjustments in a period of active economic restructuring. This could inflict irreparable damage on some sectors and could lead to the waste of Russia's precious human resources. The introduction of uniform tariffs is not recommended either and for similar reasons. All proposals which would make economic policy instruments of a rapidly changing economy rigid would hamper the creation of optimal and sustainable solutions. The example of almost all developed or developing countries indicates that the concept of a uniform tariff rate has not been excepted. In a democratic society the level of tariff protection in specific sectors is determined through bargaining between different interest groups. As a result, tariff rates differ substantially. Why should it be totally different in Russia? The argument that the appropriate democratic decisionmaking mechanism does not exist in Russia is not acceptable because one of the main points of Russian reforms is to put such mechanisms in place as soon as possible.

Therefore, the solution, which could be followed in the Russian case, would be to bind Russian tariff rates at levels, not much higher than currently applied rates, which can be justified by the degree of development of different Russian sectors. A system, with built-in flexibility should be devised, which could encourage the identification of relevant real economic interests and the development of appropriate internal economic decisionmaking mechanisms in the framework of WTO obligations. It is not in the interest of WTO members to impose tariffs on Russia which are not sustainable.

Other duties and charges levied on imports but not on domestic production (except charges for services rendered)

As shown above, Russia introduced a 3 per cent import surcharge on all goods to protect its balance-of-payments, with effect from 15 August 1998. The coverage of the surcharge was reduced in autumn 1998.

It is worthwhile noting that all Central and Eastern European GATT/WTO transition economy members have already introduced some temporary import restrictions, mainly in the form of import surcharges, for balance-of-payments reasons. This also proves that the transition process puts balance of payments under heavy pressure, an aspect of transition to be taken into account in the case of all accessions of transition economies. If accession conditions are not workable, they may contribute to balance-of-payment problems of new members leading to the WTO BOP provisions being invoked.[303]

Fees and charges for services rendered

Any fees or charges for services related to imports or exports can be imposed only in conformity with Article VIII of the GATT 1994. The basic requirement is that fees should be limited to the approximate cost of services rendered and should not represent an indirect protection to domestic products or a taxation of imports or exports for fiscal purposes. A similar commitment is included in all new protocols of accession.

The compatibility of Russia's *ad valorem* customs clearance fee with Article VIII of the GATT 1994 has been questioned in the Working Party.[304]

Application of internal taxes to imports

It is a fundamental obligation of all members to provide national treatment for imports in respect of internal taxes under Article III of the GATT. All new protocols of accession include the obligation that internal taxes should be applied to imports in full conformity with WTO requirements by the date of accession.

In Russia, besides import tariffs, there are two other types of duties applied to imported products, namely excise tax and value-added-tax (VAT). In applying these, Russia differentiates between CIS and other countries. With regard to CIS countries, VAT and excise taxes are applied upon exportation from one CIS country to another. Goods exported from CIS countries to Russia are not exempt from these taxes, but to avoid double taxation, however, VAT and excise taxes are not payable on imports into Russia unlike imports from other than CIS countries.[305] During the accession process, Russia has modified its laws on excise taxes and by the beginning of 1997 it established identical rates for imported and domestic products. Russia's draft Tax Code includes provisions that would harmonize the application of indirect taxes on imports by 2000.

Prohibitions, quotas, restrictive licences[306]

The seven finished accession procedures bear witness to the high requirements to which applicants are subjected in the area of non-tariff measures. According to the new standard practice, acceding countries, to the extent applicable, are routinely asked to accept from the date of accession the commitment to eliminate, and not introduce, reintroduce or apply quantitative restrictions on imports or other non-tariff measures such as licensing, quotas, bans, permits, prior authorization requirements, licensing requirements and other restrictions having equivalent effects which cannot be justified under the provisions of the WTO Agreements.

In Russia the legal basis for import licensing is Article 19 of the Federal Law 'On the State Regulation of Foreign Trade Activities'. Procedures for the importation of precious stones, precious metals and nuclear materials are established by Russian presidential decrees, while procedures for the importation of goods affecting Russia's national security interests and for the fulfilment of its international agreements are laid down by the Government. Russia does not use import prohibitions, which are made effective through quotas or discretionary import licensing for trade restrictive purposes. It maintains in the form of import licensing some state regulations under

Articles XX and XXI of the GATT 1994. These regulations are based on the Basel Convention and the Montreal Protocol.

Non-automatic import licenses are needed for the importation of plant protection chemicals, industrial waste, armaments, nuclear technology, precious metals, medicines, ethanol, vodka and certain other alcoholic drinks. According to the Russian authorities, in 1994 and 1995, less than one per cent of imports were subjected to import licensing.[307] Automatic import licences are required for the imports of raw and white sugar, treacle, gold and silver. From May 1998, imports of colour television sets and carpets and rugs from EU countries became subject to automatic licensing. According to the Russian authorities, licensing does not impose any quantitative or other restrictions on imports: its purpose is to ensure adequate governmental control over imports of goods which may represent a threat to the country's national security or jeopardise life and health, the fauna and flora, or the environment. In some cases the purpose of licensing is to monitor imports and, in the case of colour television sets, to combat smuggling. The operation of the licensing system is based on Articles VIII (Fees and Formalities connected with Importation and Exportation), X (Publication and Administration of Trade Regulations), XX (General Exceptions) and XXI (Security Exceptions) of the GATT 1994.

Import licensing procedures

In Russia all individuals and legal entities resident in the country are eligible to apply for licenses. Import licenses are granted by the Ministry of Foreign Economic Relations, but applicants must first obtain consent from the specific relevant ministry or authority (for example, from the Ministry of Atomic Power in the case of nuclear materials). According to the rules, the license issue period may not exceed 21 days. An application for a license may be refused if the importation of the product would violate national security interests, international obligations, or represent a threat to the life and health of the population, wildlife, plants, or the environment. The reasons for any refusal are given to the applicant in writing, and may be appealed against in court. A licence is issued for a rouble fee in an amount equal to US$ 150; its validity may not exceed 12 months and licences are not transferable. Foreign exchange for goods to be imported is automatically provided by the importer's bank.

Customs valuation

The importance of customs valuation is shown by the fact that customs procedures may be used as non-tariff barriers if goods are incorrectly classified as this may lead to the imposition of higher tariffs. It is obvious that such practices might make tariff reductions and tariff bindings meaningless. The basic rules on customs valuation are contained in Article VII of the GATT. In light of certain questionable national practices, during the Tokyo Round an Agreement on Interpretation of Article VII was adopted with the purpose of making the rules on customs valuation more uniform and transparent. The Agreement sets out five valuations methods, which are ranked, in a hierarchical order to be followed by national customs administrations. The primary basis for customs value under the Agreement is 'transaction value', which is defined by Article I of the Agreement as 'the price actually paid or payable for the goods when sold for export to the country of importation'. When the customs value can not be established under Article I, Article II should be applied which includes different additional valuation methods. The Agreement was not signed by most developing countries because they considered that it unduly inhibited their national customs administrations in dealing with the widespread practice of under-invoicing goods in order to reduce the amount of customs duties to be paid. This issue has been addressed by a Ministerial Decision adopted during the Uruguay Round which provides that 'where the customs administration has reason to doubt the truth or accuracy of the particulars or of documents produced in support' of declaration, 'the customs administration may ask the importer to provide further explanation, including documents or other evidence.'[308] If the authorities still remain unsatisfied, they have the right to move from the transaction value to other valuation methods defined by the Agreement. Developing countries, many of which use valuation methods based on officially established minimum values incompatible with the Agreement, have been given a period of five years to implement the provisions of the Agreement. Upon request, this period may be extended by the Committee on Customs Valuation.

Recent accession protocols indicate that all newly acceded countries undertook to apply fully, without recourse to a transition period, the WTO provisions concerning customs valuation from the date of their accession. Ecuador and Panama agreed to eliminate the use of 'minimum values for customs purposes' or 'minimum import prices'.

In Russia, the Law on Customs Tariff and other rules which govern customs valuation are not based on the WTO Agreement, but most of the written regulations are not far from WTO rules. Again, the problem is with the implementation of the legal regulations. There are many complaints that Russian customs regulations change frequently and 'are subject to arbitrary application by each port of entry, and can be burdensome.'[309] Customs practices are often described as 'complex and frequently confused' or arbitrary, and customs officials as incompetent, slow and corrupt. Most concerns were expressed about the implementation of customs legislation rather than the legislation itself.[310]

Given the importance, it is very probable that members will insist that Russia should also undertake to apply WTO provisions on customs valuation from the date of its accession, without any transition period. How problems related to implementation can be solved in the framework of the protocol of accession, remains an open question.

Anti-dumping, countervailing, safeguard regimes

The application of the WTO Agreement on Safeguards, the Agreement on Implementation of Article VI of the GATT 1994 (Anti-dumping) and the Agreement on Subsidies and Countervailing Measures is optional in that members are not obliged to apply them or adopt related national legislation. But if a country decides to use such protective measures, it is obliged to proceed in accordance with the provisions of these agreements.

It is evident that the requirements of WTO members *vis-à-vis* new applicants in the area of contingency protection agreements have also become stricter in recent years. In the case of earlier accessions (Ecuador and Bulgaria) members accepted the possibility that anti-dumping or countervailing duty actions might be taken even in the absence of relevant national legislation on condition that, from the date of accession, these proceedings and measures were administered in full conformity with the relevant WTO Agreements. The last three accession protocols, however, provide that in the absence of appropriate national legislation no anti-dumping, countervailing duty or safeguard measures can be taken until such legislation, in conformity with the provisions of these WTO Agreements, has been implemented. This means that these new members, without explicit WTO obligation to do so, have given up their rights to use such measures until they adopt appropriate national legislation.[311] It should be added, however, that in practical terms linking contingency protection measures and the adoption of appropriate national laws is not excessive because the direct application of these WTO Agreements without appropriate national implementing regulations would be very difficult, especially for transition economies with underdeveloped trade administrations.

Russia's accession conditions concerning contingency protection measures will be different from those of other transition economies as, in April 1998, a Federal Law was adopted entitled 'On Measures to Protect the Economic Interests of the Russian Federation in Foreign Trade in Goods'.[312] The Russian Working Party has already started examining the new Law from the point of view of its compatibility with WTO provisions. The Law covers substantive and procedural aspects of the imposition of safeguard, anti-dumping and countervailing measures. It also includes rules on import restrictions taken for balance-of-payments reasons; the fulfilling of federal development programmes aimed at the introduction of new products; protection of industries undergoing restructuring and the protection of agricultural production. Investigations under the Law are to be conducted by the Ministry of Trade.

In July 1998, Russia imposed temporary special duties on raw and white sugar imports on the basis of Article 6 of the Law (Application of Safeguard measures).[313] The purpose of the safeguard measure was to prevent a threat of substantial damage to the domestic sugar industry due to a sharp increase in raw and white sugar imports. The measure was revoked in early 1999.

According to Article 15:2 of the Law, import restrictions for the purpose of safeguarding the balance of payments, subject to Russia's international obligations, are to be implemented through import quotas, or other measures, for the period necessary to restore the balance of payments. During the examination of the Law in the Working Party, questions can be expected on the compatibility of using import quotas for balance-of-payment purposes as the provisions of the 'Understanding on the Balance-of-Payments Provisions of the GATT 1994' require the use of price-based measures such as import surcharges, import deposit requirements or 'other equivalent trade measures with an impact on the price of imported goods'.[314] The imposition of new quantitative restrictions for balance-of-payments purposes is to be avoided unless, 'because of a critical balance-of-payments situation, price-based measures cannot arrest a sharp deterioration in the external payments position.'[315]

Article 16:1 of the Law provides that the introduction of new products originating from federal development programmes or restructuring Russian industries may be protected against import competition through the introduction of import quotas 'for a period necessary to achieve the said objectives, provided such period does not exceed four years.' According to Article 16:2, import quotas for the protection of the domestic agricultural market may be introduced by the Federal government for a period not exceeding one year. Obviously, Russia attaches great importance to these protective measures aimed at facilitating economic restructuring at this difficult stage in the country's economic transition process. It remains to be seen to what extent members can tolerate deviations from established WTO rules. Experience of earlier accession processes suggests that the level of tolerance has become much lower over the last couple of years.

Policies affecting trade in goods (exports)

At the very beginning of the transition process, between 1992 and 1995, Russia used tariff and non-tariff export control measures extensively, mainly due to huge differences between Russian and world price levels. Most exports were subject to tariffs, quotas, and licensing and mandatory contract registration. By the end of 1995, most export control measures had been eliminated.

Customs tariffs, fees and charges for services rendered and application of internal taxes to exports

Provisions of the WTO Agreement, subject to certain conditions, allow members to levy duties on exports if these are deemed necessary to control exports or achieve important policy objectives. Accession protocols of Mongolia, Bulgaria, the Kyrgyz Republic, Latvia and Estonia show that these countries maintained some sort of customs tariffs on exports during the period of their accession negotiation. Their protocols of accession clearly reflect the strong expectations of WTO members that acceding countries reduce the use of export taxes and tariffs. As a result, Bulgaria and Estonia undertook to minimize the use of export taxes while Latvia and Mongolia committed themselves to abolish all export duties by 2000 and 2006 respectively.

In 1992, in the context of the a very bureaucratic export policy described above, Russia replaced export taxes levied by the former Soviet Union with export customs duties. The main purpose of levying export tariffs was to reduce the differences between the administratively controlled low domestic prices of Russia's main export commodities and world prices. As mentioned earlier, the huge differences between external and internal prices was the basis of private fortunes being made by criminals and mafias. Export duty was levied on 150 commodity items which included certain raw materials, ferrous and non ferrous metals, chemicals, timber products, foodstuffs, aviation engineering products, armaments and military materials. In value terms, about 75 per cent of Russian exports were subject to these frequently changing *ad valorem* and specific export duties.

By the end of 1995, the gap between Russian and world prices for many traditional export items considerably narrowed or disappeared, leading to the lowering or elimination of most export tariffs. Export tariffs were later imposed for fiscal reasons. In April 1996, export duties were lifted on all types of goods.[316] After the crash of 17 August 1998, Russia reintroduced export duties on a number of strategic export products. According to the Russian trade minister, the introduction of export duties was only a 'temporary measure. Export should prevent domestic prices from rising and increase tax revenues at a time of economic stabilization.'[317] With effect from 1 August 1999, the government introduced a customs tax of 5 Euro/1000 kg on crude oil exported outside the customs union.[318] It is the declared intention of the government to review and abolish export restrictions, dependent on the country's financial position and not to impose new quantitative restrictions on international trade.[319] Russian goods exported outside the CIS are exempted from VAT and excise duties except oil and liquefied natural gas which are subject to excise duties at differentiated rates. Russian exports to CIS countries are liable to VAT.

It can be expected that Russia, similarly to other newly acceded countries will be asked to undertake the abolition of export duties, or at least minimize the use of them.

Export restrictions

Between 1992 and 1995, Russia, for economic reasons, maintained a comprehensive system of administrative export restrictions (as we have shown earlier, the system was unworkable and was rightly criticized for promoting corruption). About 82 per cent of Russian exports were subject to export licensing, of which 72 per cent were also covered by export quotas.[320] As monitoring exports became more and more difficult, the right to export strategic goods was restricted to a limited group ('special exporters') from July 1992 which covered about 70 per cent of the country's exports. Export contracts for certain categories of goods, for the purpose of export price controls, were also liable to mandatory registration. From 1993, administrative export controls were gradually phased out. By 1995, the mandatory registration of export contracts, together with export restrictions on strategically important raw materials were eliminated. By the end of 1995, only about 10 per cent of Russian exports were subject to licences, and this was for reasons of national security, the protection of the environment or the fulfilment of international obligations. In October 1998, the exportation of oilseeds and raw hides and skins became subjected to automatic licensing.

Export subsidies

Russia considers that it's state export support system, which is based on the 'Federal Exports Development Programme until the year 2005', put into effect by Government Resolution No.123 'On the Federal Exports Development Programme' of 8 February 1996, is in compliance with the WTO Agreement on Subsidies and Countervailing measures.[321] The forms of government assistance include providing information on foreign markets, data on trade legislation of other countries and providing support in avoiding trade conflicts and disputes.

Internal policies affecting foreign trade in goods

Industrial policy, subsidies

Rules of the WTO system do not directly address the question of industrial policy, but they cover a number of trade and economic policy instruments such as subsidies, price controls, trade restrictions, tax regimes, economy-related regulatory systems and government procurement, which can be considered as constituent parts of an industrial policy.[322] According to neo-liberal orthodoxy, there is no need for a state industrial policy because resources should be allocated by the market alone. While the theory has solid foundations in general, it's implementation in specific countries raises many questions also in well-functioning market economies. Consequently, even in these countries, some sort of industrial policy can be found. In the case of transition economies the special problem is that they need quick resource allocation, but economic units, due to the underdeveloped nature of the market, do not respond appropriately to market signals, and as a result resource allocation is slow and distorted. In such imperfect situations the basic question is not whether the state should or should not intervene but rather, what of state intervention is necessary to correct the imperfect situation.[323]

At the beginning of its reform process, Russia did not have a clearly defined industrial policy because having one was not found to be compatible with its radical market economy reforms. Reformers did their best to shrink the role of the state in economic management. As we saw, however, the government gave support in an inconsistent way in the form of direct payments, tax concessions, tax deferrals and soft loans to whole sectors or individual enterprises. The first comprehensive Russian industrial policy concept was embodied in 'Russian Economic Reform and Development in 1995–1997' and in the 'Industrial Policy Guidelines for 1995–1997', both approved, against the background of the acute industrial crises, by the government and the Commission on Operational Matters in April 1995. Measures for the industrial policy included a 'System of State Regulation of Industrial Production' and 'Structural and Investment Policies in Industry'.

Industrial Policy Guidelines for 1995–97 provide for: streamlining the system of government regulation in industry; reforming the economic environment; implementing organizational and institutional change in industry, including privatization, the reorganization of inefficient enterprises, incentives for the creation of financial and industrial groups and the support for free enterprise in industrial production; pursuing active structural and investment policies, including the conversion of defence industries to civilian output; establishing an infrastructure for commodity markets; encouraging innovation and scientific and technological development in industry; forming and implementing vigorous industrial policies at the subfederal level; promoting co-operation in industry with other CIS countries and Central and Eastern European nations; ensuring Russia's integration into the world economy; creating new jobs and training personnel in industry.[324] The main objective of the Russian industrial policy is to create a diversified, high-tech and competitive industry which can guarantee the strengthening of the country's economic independence and national security, a high standard of living, a healthy economic environment and the integration of the country into the global economy under equal and mutually favourable conditions.[325]

Russia also provides state support for small business at federal, regional and local levels. The areas to which state support is directed are set out in Article 6 of the Federal law 'On State Support for Small Business in the Russian Federation'. Support for small business is not based on providing state financial assistance to various entrepreneurs but on the development of generally favourable conditions for entrepreneurial activity in the form of legal protection, the development of business services through specialized organizations supported by the state and business associations.[326]

After the August 1998 crisis the mood in government circles shifted towards a more interventionist approach in economic policy matters. New requirements were formulated based on increasing the role of the state in economic management, developing the real sector of the economy and concentrating on specific sectors which included both high-tech and traditional sectors, such as the light industry and food industries.[327] It is important to note, however, that due to lack of resources this new policy has not been translated into meaningful concrete economic measures. But budgetary austerity has increased the temptation of using foreign trade related measures for both industrial policy and budgetary reasons. The depreciation of the rouble has resulted in the contraction of imports and facilitated the development of import substitution and has given a stimulus to exports. Until now Russia has avoided to increasing import barriers but has imposed taxes on windfall profits made by energy and primary commodities exporters.

Article VI of the GATT 1994, as elaborated by the Agreement on Subsidies and Countervailing Measures, sets out important rules on subsidies covering industrial products. The Agreement recognizes the right of WTO members to use subsidies to achieve various political objectives, but it imposes restraints on administrations to grant subsidies that have significant trade distorting effects. The Agreement categorizes subsidies into prohibited and permissible subsidies. Export subsidies and other subsidies which are contingent upon the use of domestic over imported goods, are prohibited. According to Article 29, transition economies may apply programmes and measures necessary for economic transformation but have a transition period of seven years, starting from the date of entry into force of the Agreement, within which they are under the obligation to phase out their prohibited subsidies or bring them into conformity with the Agreement. All other subsidies, which are not prohibited, are permissible.[328] Permissible subsidies may be actionable or not actionable. The Agreement lays down a complex system of rules on substantive and procedural aspects of the remedies available to importing countries.[329]

The debate over whether to give or not to give transition periods to acceding countries for the fulfilment of certain specific WTO obligations is also highly relevant in subsidy-related matters. Developing country members are mostly in favour of transition periods making reference to Article 27 and 29 of the Agreement. Some developed countries, however, oppose it, arguing that transition periods provided for in the WTO Agreements, which are anyway expiring, were accorded to original members only in order to help them become accustomed to their new obligations. Acceding governments are in a different position, as they knew the requirements of the different WTO Agreements since their entry into force. Therefore, transition periods included in WTO Agreements are not applicable automatically to acceding governments. Some other members said that they were not, *a priori*, opposed to transitional periods, provided that there was a clear justification for them.[330]

Among the newly acceded members Ecuador, Mongolia, Panama and the Kyrgyz Republic maintained prohibited subsidies at the time of their accession. Ecuador undertook the elimination of all such subsidies before its accession, while the other three countries are obliged to eliminate all subsidies inconsistent with Article 3 of the Agreement by 31 December 2002, a date which corresponds to the expiry of the seven years transition period provided by the Agreement.

At present, according to the authorities, Russia does not provide prohibited subsidies.[331] Other subsidies it does grant include:[332]

a) Direct transfers from the Federal Budget (10.7 per cent of total subsidies). These subsidies are mainly granted to the coal sector and the military industry for reorientation and modernization of disengaged industrial facilities; b) Budgetary loans for Enterprises and Organizations (4.3 per cent of total subsidies). The loans are repayable, the wood industry was the main beneficiary; c) deferred payments to the Federal Budget, to stabilize the financial conditions of certain industrial enterprises (4.8 per cent of total subsidies); d) investment tax credits, on an interest-bearing and non-forgiveable basis (0.04 per cent of total subsidies); e) Specific Form of State Support, to help eliminate the consequences of natural calamities, fires and disasters (1.3 per cent of total subsidies); f) Grants and Subsidies to Regions. These subsidies represent the biggest part of Russia's subsidies programme (62 per cent of total subsidies); g) State Financing for Specific Programmes.[333] Russia has started to develop its export insurance system with the promise that it will fully comply with the provisions, including Annex I, of the Agreement. The Russian subsidy system and its effect on trade are still the subject of thorough examination in the Working Party. It can be expected that Russia will be asked to phase out all subsidies found to be incompatible with the provisions of the Agreement.

Technical barriers to trade, sanitary and phytosanitary measures

Voluntary and mandatory standards (technical regulations) as well as certification systems are adopted for the protection of the health and safety of people and for the preservation of the environment. The WTO Agreement on Technical Barriers to Trade (TBT Agreement) recognizes the rights of member states to take such measures subject to the requirement that they are neither applied in a manner which would constitute a means of arbitrary or unjustifiable discrimination between countries where the same conditions prevail nor as disguised restrictions on international trade. The TBT Agreement lays down detailed rules with the objective of ensuring that technical regulations and other standards and certification systems do not create unnecessary barriers to trade. One way of achieving this objective is to ensure these measures are based on international standards. Countries also require that imported agricultural items comply with their sanitary and phytosanitary regulations. The aim of these regulations is to protect human, animal or plant life or health from pests and diseases that might be brought in by imported products. The object-ive of the WTO Agreement on the Application of Sanitary and Phy-tosanitary Measures (SPS Agreement) is, similarly to the TBT Agreement's objective, to further the use of harmonized sanitary and phytosanitary measures between members based on interna-tional standards, guidelines and recommendations developed by international organizations.

Newly acceded countries, with the exception of the Kyrgyz Repub-lic, in respect of the SPS Agreement, agreed to apply the TBT and SPS Agreements from the date of accession, without recourse to any transitional period. In the Kyrgyz Republic sanitary and phytosanit-ary standards were not in full conformity with the WTO require-ments, which meant the country had to accept the obligation to report annually on progress in the work on harmonization of its standards with international standards until conformity with WTO requirements is achived. There are cases where the obligations of new members go beyond the obligations included in the Agreements. For example, Bulgaria accepted that it 'will not require additional certifi-cation or sanitary registration for products which have been certified as safe for human use and consumption by recognized foreign or international bodies.' The Kyrgyz Republic has also undertaken a similar obligation. The Agreements do not provide for such a strict obligation.

Business people often criticize Russia's standards, testing, certifica-tion and labelling procedures stating that they have become a sig-nificant obstacle to market access. Russia's consumer protection law requires official certification of imported products for conformity to Russian technical, safety and quality standards. Certification is based on a combination of international and Russian standards. Similar requirements are also imposed at the city and district level and run counter to federal legislation, (in this respect the Moscow alcohol decree case is mentioned). In addition, US, and also European com-panies, have complained of costly procedures and arbitrary certifica-tion practices for many products, particularly telecommunication equipment.[334]

The issue of TBTs and SPS measures has been on the agenda of the Working Party almost since the beginning of the accession process.[335] Members of the Working Party have raised many questions on both Russia's relevant legislation and its practice. It was recognized that one of the root causes of problems was that Russia still applied a relatively small proportion (33 per cent) of international standards. Russia justifies deviations from international standards with arguments stressing her different geographical, climatic and other conditions, and pointing out that the treatment accorded to foreign products is not less favourable than that accorded to like domestic products. Members urged Russia to increase the proportion of international standards used. Criticism was expressed of Government Resolution No.1575, which requires mandatory labelling of food products in Russian, especially because of the short time limit (one month) specified for compliance. The implementation of the Resolution has been postponed several times. A similar requirement is applied on non-food products based on Government Resolution 1037. And similarly, the reasonability of the requirement to affix holographic marks to some products (alcoholic beverages and audio-visual products) was questioned. The conformity of the Russian certificate and testing systems with the TBT Agreement was also discussed. It was understood that Russia had serious problems in complying with the requirements of the TBT Agreement. What has come out of the discussion is that Russia needs more time to establish an appropriate enquiry point which could provide information in TBT and SPS matters. There are still many questions regarding Russia's compliance with international standards in the area of SPS measures. In view of many unresolved questions, and the lack of transparency regarding legislation and practice, there can be no doubt that the Working Party should continue its work in many TBT and SPS-related issues.

Trade-related investment measures

Trade-related investment measures (TRIMs), such as local content requirements or export performance requirements, are frequently used by developing countries to influence the market behaviour of foreign investors. The Agreement on Trade-related Investment Measures (TRIMs Agreement), which was concluded during the Uruguay Round, due to the resistance of developing countries, does not address all aspects of the complex issue of such measures and certainly does not cover the area of investment in general. For this reason, it prohibits countries from using the five specified TRIMs which specifically violate GATT provisions, namely Article III (national treatment) and XI (prohibition on the use of quantitative restrictions). The prohibited TRIMs include local content requirements, trade-balancing requirements, foreign exchange balancing requirements, exchange restrictions and domestic sales requirements.[336] Developing country members have been given a grace period of five years from 1 January 1995 to phase out the TRIMs which are inconsistent with the TRIMs Agreement.

Out of the seven countries that have finished accession negotiations with the WTO, only Ecuador maintained TRIMs that were inconsistent with the provisions of the TRIMs Agreement. Ecuador accepted the commitment to phase out such measures prior to 1 January 2000. The other countries either did not maintain measures that were not in conformity with the TRIMs Agreement or, if they did, they undertook the obligation to achieve full consistency upon accession.

The basis of Russia's foreign investment regime is the 1991 Law 'On Foreign Investment in the Russian Federation'. Russia applies to foreign investors a 'national treatment regime with exemptions'. Foreign investments are not subject to special licensing but more than 70 types of activity are liable to licensing at federal, regional and local levels. In the case of insurance activity, foreigners can invest no more than 49 per cent of the authorized capital. In banking services, the share of foreign capital in the total capital of the Russian banking system may not exceed 12 per cent. There are also activities which can be carried out only by state enterprises. These include the manufacture and production of narcotic and poisonous substances, processing of precious metals, ores, making and processing radioactive and rare-earth elements, making government honours and medals, the sale of precious metals on external markets and the sale of native diamonds and rough gemstones. Only state enterprises may be users of minerals for the extraction of radioactive raw materials. There are also some bans and other restrictions imposed on foreign investors for national security and other reasons. A further very important restriction is that land may not be sold to foreign corporations or individuals.

The level of foreign investments for the size and potential of the country, is very low. There is no doubt that this is due to the fact that Russia is a country of very high investment risk. In 1998, the value of foreign investments, after the peak year of 1997 (US$6.2 billion), fell back to its 1995 level, US$2.2 billion, remaining much behind the US$10–12 billion level foreseen by the country's 'Long-term guidelines of the foreign investment policy'.[337] According to foreign observers, 'the principal limitations to foreign investment in Russia are macroeconomic instability, ambiguity with respect to future investment policies and the lack of a transparent and stable legal structure.' Requirements can be confusing and burdensome for investors, bureaucratic discretion may be erratic and the business infrastructure is poorly developed. Only a few incentives are offered to foreign investors. Some of them, like certain tax benefits, have never been implemented. A major complaint made by foreign investors is about the large number of taxes and the lack of stability and transparency of the system.[338]

Based on Russia's law 'On Production Sharing Agreements', adopted at the end of 1995, the country concluded a number production sharing agreements with foreign investors to regulate the extraction of natural resources. In principle, the major advantage of production sharing agreements is that they place tax and other conditions of individual investment projects on a long-term contractual basis, thus removing the unpredictability of the investment system. In practice, however, it has turned out that the process of approval of such agreements was long and complicated; that the language of the legislation raised the risk of arbitrary interpretations of the definition of 'essential change in the circumstances'; and that there was a lack of an adequate implementing legislation.[339]

In light of the many problems associated with foreign investment, a new draft law 'On Foreign Investment in the Russian Federation' was worked out. The draft includes guarantees, at least for seven years, against the main danger in the Russian investment regime, the unpredictable and unfavourable changes in regulations. The draft was adopted by the Duma in April 1999, but the Federation Council rejected it in the following month. According to some comments, the reason for the rejection was that 'the law will give preference to foreign investors to the detriments of domestic producers.'[340]

The Working Party has discussed all aspects of Russia's foreign investment regime. This broad approach has been questioned on the basis that CIS acceding countries 'have been asked to provide extensive information on their foreign investment laws, going much beyond the scope of the TRIMs Agreement.'[341] Russia stated that its 'national legislation currently in effect contains no general trade-related investment measures inconsistent with the requirements of the TRIMs Agreement.' It recognized, however, that Article 7:2 of the law 'On Production Sharing Agreements' legally obliged the parties to purchase at least a certain portion of machinery and services from domestic suppliers.[342] In July 1998, Government Resolution No.716, in the case of the importation of leased aircraft of foreign origin, provides for some VAT and customs duty preferences on condition that the importer will buy or lease Russian made aircraft to a value which exceeds the preferences granted by up to three times.[343]

Russia has declared its intent to observe the provisions of the TRIMs Agreement, but it left the question of an eventual transition period open.[344] In light of previous protocols of accession it can be taken for granted that WTO members would like Russia to comply with the provisions of the TRIMS Agreement by the time of its accession to the organization.

State trading entities

Article XVII of the GATT 1947 recognized that state enterprises with exclusive or special privileges might be operated so as to create serious obstacles to trade. Therefore, it laid down certain rules on the functioning of such enterprises. However, Article XVII of the GATT 1947 did not provide a clear definition of state trading and thereby made room for different, often contradictory, interpretations.[345] In order to ensure transparency in the activities of state trading enterprises, the 'Understanding on the Interpretation of Article XVII of the GATT 1994' established a new system of notification and gave the following working definition of state trading enterprises: 'Governmental and non-governmental enterprises, including marketing boards, which have been granted exclusive or special rights or privileges, including statutory or constitutional powers, in the exercise of which they influence through their purchases or sales the level or direction of imports or exports.'

The GATT 1994 imposes the obligation on members to ensure that state trading organizations act in a manner consistent with the general principles of nondiscrimination. This means that purchases or sales by state trading enterprises should be made in accordance with commercial considerations and that adequate opportunities should be provided to enterprises in other countries to compete for participation in purchases and sales involving state trading enterprises. Article VIII of the GATS (Monopolies and Exclusive Service Suppliers) includes similar provisions on monopoly and exclusive suppliers of services.[346]

All protocols of accession of transition economies include the obligation that the new members apply their laws and regulations governing the trading activities of state-owned enterprises and other enterprises with special or exclusive privileges and that such enterprises act in full conformity with the provisions of the WTO Agreement, in particular Article XII of the GATT 1994 and the Understanding on that Article and Article VIII of the GATS. In addition to this commitment, Estonia confirmed that it was the government's intent to 'eventually eliminate its State trading role'.

At the beginning of the accession process, Russia reported to the Working Party that none of it's enterprises were covered by Article XVII of the GATT 1994.[347] Some months later, in early 1996, Russia informed the Working Party that after a careful review of developments and the relevant WTO rules it had established a preliminary list of ten enterprises which should be notified under Article XVII.[348] In 1997, reflecting a substantial uncertainty in the interpretation of the relevant rules, Russia announced that 'nine out of ten enterprises enumerated...do not enjoy these privileges any more.[349] On the other hand, after carrying out additional examination in terms of Article XVII of GATT 1994 and the working definition of State-Trading Enterprises in the Understanding on the Interpretation of that Article, four other enterprises were identified as 'possible State-Trading Enterprises'.[350] Out of these five state-trading enterprises, four are joint stock companies: Gazprom (natural gas); United Energy Service of Russia (UES (electricity)); Rosugol (coal); ALROSA (raw natural diamonds) and Almazyuvelir Export Foreign Trade Association is a state enterprise.

Gazprom's special privilege in terms of Article XVII is that it has licenses to develop 92 gas and gas condensate fields and owns 100 per cent of Russia's grid of high-pressure pipelines. According to Russia, export prices are established by Gazprom, the world largest gas company, on the basis of market principles. Export prices for natural gas are much higher than domestic prices, which are regulated and kept down for social reasons by the State.

UES of Russia owns the vast majority of Russia's power generating facilities and 100 per cent of the country's power grid, giving it a total monopoly of electricity transfer. Export prices are determined by UES on the basis of market principles. Export prices are higher than prices on the domestic market. Both Gazprom and UES have the right to export and import gas and electricity, respectively. Both companies have almost complete monopoly of their industries' infrastructure. Free competition can not exist in these areas. (In 1997, a government resolution authorized, to a certain capacity, the use of gas pipelines owned by Gazprom for other exporters of gas.)

Rosugol's special privilege was the distribution of government subsidies for coal mining and it played an important role in the determination of freight rates for the transportation of coal. However, in November 1997, Rosugol was dissolved. Its administrative tasks were transferred to the Ministry of Fuel and Energy and its commercial and other business functions given to two joint stock companies. The special privilege of ALROSA and Almazyuvelirexport is the exclusive right to export raw diamonds. Export prices are determined by ALROSA and other producers. Exports of raw natural diamonds are subject to quotas established by the government, while imports are free also for private traders.

The list of Russian state-trading enterprises implies that, according to the authorities, at present, there are no functioning state-trading entities in agriculture and, as was declared, 'The Government of the Russian Federation does not have intentions to introduce state trading for agricultural products in the future.'[351] Until 1995, Roskhlebo-product, later the Federal Food Corporation (FFC) executed the functions of state contractor for grains, sugar beet, oilseeds, linen and some other products. However, in September 1997, the FFC was liquidated and at the same time the Federal Agency for Food Market Regulation was established with the functions of monitoring agricultural markets, promoting competition and commodity investments and, through the involvement of commercial entities, act as a state customer in respect of state food reserves. According to the Russian authorities, the Agency is not a state-trading entity in terms of Article XVII of the GATT 1994.

According to estimates, the total value of state trading activity in 1997 for Russia was US$36.9 billion, or 26.5 per cent of total trade. This estimates, however, includes the US$10 billion trade turnover of the country's state-owned or state controlled foreign trade organizations which are not included in the list of state-trading entities provided by Russia. According to the same source, the value of state trading was expected to fall to about 14–16 per cent of total trade.[352] This share may still be considered substantial, but it should be recognized that in Russia the level of state influence in foreign trade has been diminished by historically unprecedented proportions within a very short period of time. The confusion about the criteria of what constitutes state trading and the lack of transparency in relations between the state and some trading entities had much to do with the absence of a consistent economic reform concept. It can be expected that with the advancement of reforms, the status and privileges of trading entities will be clarified and Russia will be ready, as were new WTO members, to observe WTO provisions in the area of state trading.

Government procurement

Article III:8(a) and XVII:2 of the GATT 1947 exempted procurements by governmental agencies for governmental purposes from national treatment and most favoured nation treatment obligations. The purpose behind this regulation was to maintain the right of governments to give preferential treatment to domestic producers in the large market of government procurement.[353] However, the practice of buying local products and services even though foreign supplies were available at lower prices increased government expenditure and decreased economic efficiency. These and some other considerations led the contracting parties of the GATT to negotiate, in the Tokyo Round, an Agreement on Government Procurement. This Agreement, which covered only goods, required national treatment and nondiscrimination for purchases by government entities and established detailed rules on tendering procedures. The Agreement was applied only to signatories and entities which were included in country schedules. During the Uruguay Round the scope of the Agreement was expanded by new types of entities (sub-central government entities and public utilities) and by the inclusion of services and construction. As the Agreement on Government Procurement is a 'plurilateral' agreement and not part of the 'single undertaking', only those WTO members which sign it separately become party to it. In June 1999, the Agreement had 27 seven members, practically all of them developed economies.

All new accession protocols contain fairly stringent conditions on government procurements. While Mongolia only made the commitment to seek observer status in the Committee for the Agreement on Government Procurement at the time of it's accession, 'with a view to initiating negotiations for membership thereafter', the commitments of most other countries are time bound, indicating the date for the tabling of an entity offer and the expected date for the completion of negotiations for membership in the Agreement.[354] Because of the pressure exerted on acceding governments in the Working Party to join the Agreement on Government Procurement and also the Agreement on Trade in Civil Aircraft, several WTO members expressed dissatisfaction, stating that membership in plurilateral agreements 'should not be made a condition of accession to the WTO, as Article XII itself made it quite clear that the procedures for accession to these were quite separate from accession to the WTO itself.'[355]

The importance of government procurements in Russia can be demonstrated by its volume. According to Russian estimations federal budgetary allocations for purchases to meet state needs vary between 7 to 12 per cent of the GNP. However, laws, regulations and state practices related to government procurement, for understandable historical reasons, are still poorly developed. At the beginning of the accession process, Russia declared that from the points of view of purchases for state needs 'there are no advantages for domestic Russian suppliers compared to foreign ones.'[356] Federal Law 'On deliveries of Products for Federal State Needs' of 1995 made no distinction between government procurement and purchases for resale to the general population. Both fell under the category 'purchases for state needs'. In making purchases for state needs, the Law introduced a 'general prohibition on the purchase of foreign made products unless the purchase of the Russian equivalent is impossible or economically inexpedient'[357]. Foreign tenderers in the Russian government procurement market face some product-specific preferences established in favour of domestic companies in the area of farm products, raw materials and foodstuffs for government use and construction. (When a foreign construction company wins a tender to build a facility with government financing, Government Decision No.531 of 8 June 1993 requires that a maximum amount of domestic equipment and material should be employed by such contractors and that not less than 30 per cent of labour and other service contracts should be awarded to Russian subcontractors.)

According to information given by Russian authorities, a draft Federal Law 'On the Organization of Tenders for the Purchases of Goods, Building Works, and Services to Meet State Needs' is based, among others, on the GATT Agreement on Government Procurement. 'If enacted, the law will establish general legal and economic principles for organizing tenders for the purchase of goods, building works, and services to satisfy State needs.'[358] Pending the approval of the draft law, Presidential decree No.305 of 8 April 1997 'On Measurement to Prevent Corruption and Budget Expenses Cutback in Organization of Purchase of Goods' was adopted which lays down basis rules on tender procedures. The Decree, which remains in force until the draft law is adopted, makes tendering procedures more transparent and open for foreigners with the exception of government procurements related to national security.

It is not easy to get reliable information on the implementation of the rules of government procurement in Russia. All available information suggests that corruption is also pervasive in this area. According to estimates, 'no less than 70 per cent of all officials are corrupt'. According to the same source, in 1997, 16.4 thousand crimes against the government and the interests of public service were registered, 11.4 per cent more than in 1996.[359] As stated by a relevant study, 'Corruption has become a way of life for Government officials in Russia.'[360] Russia has recognized that corruption in government procurement constitutes a major problem. One of the objectives of Presidential Decree No.305 is to fight it in this area through improving the relevant procedures and building appropriate new institutions in accordance with international practice.

Based on already established WTO practice, it can be expected that Russia, similarly to other acceding governments, will also be asked to initiate negotiations upon accession for membership in the Government Procurement Agreement and complete them by a fixed date.

Trade in civil aircraft

The WTO Civil Aircraft Agreement is one of the plurilateral agreements. It binds only the signatories, who include all major aircraft exporters except Russia. The aim of the Agreement is to reduce tariffs and non-tariff barriers affecting trade in civil aircraft. Russia has a relatively developed aircraft industry with substantial production capacities. At the same time Russia also constitutes a huge market, as over the next 20 years it will need as many as 1600 aircraft. In 1996, in a Memorandum of Understanding with the United States, Russia has undertaken to progressively reduce import tariffs on aircraft. It can be taken for granted that Russia will be asked to become signatory to the Agreement upon accession to the WTO. Even acceding countries with marginal importance in that sector like the Kyrgyz Republic, Latvia and Estonia were asked to accept this commitment. This practice, however, was criticized by some members stating that adherence to the plurilateral agreements was not a precondition for accession.[361] Russia has not yet taken a definite position on its eventual membership in the Agreement, referring to the substantial changes which are taking place in its aircraft sector. It stated, however, that 'We do not link the conditions of our accession to the WTO with accession to the Agreement on Trade in Civil Aircraft'.[362]

Agricultural commitments

WTO rules on agriculture

Rules of the GATT 1947 treated trade in agricultural products differently to trade in manufactures. Disciplines for agriculture prohibed neither quantitative restrictions nor export subsidies, while the use of these trade policy instruments were forbidden in trade in industrial products. A major achievement of the Uruguay Round was that the Agreement on Agriculture has established a framework for bringing trade in agricultural products under normal GATT discipline.

The Agreement is based on three main pillars, namely: market access commitments; a commitment to bind and reduce support to domestic producers of agricultural products; the binding and reduction of export subsidies. Under the rules relating to market access commitments, members were required to abolish such non-tariff measures as quantitative restrictions, discretionary licensing and variable levies by calculating their tariff equivalents and adding these to the fixed tariffs. Members have undertaken to bind these new tariff rates and reduce them by an average 37 per cent by developed countries and 24 per cent by developing countries, within six and ten years respectively. (Least developed countries are not required to reduce their bound tariffs.) The Agreement does not include specific provisions for transition economies.[363] As a result of tariffication, the new tariff rates are rather high, generally ranging between 60 and 100 per cent, with some tariff peaks over 300 per cent.

The Agreement divides subsidies into two groups. Green subsidies, which have no, or at most minimal, trade distorting effects or effects on production, and do not provide price support to producers.[364] These subsidies are not covered by reduction commitment. And amber subsidies which encompass subsidies to which reduction commitments apply, that is mainly domestic support subsidies. Total domestic support, which includes both border and non-border policy measures, is subject to a ceiling which is calculated on a product by product basis as the Aggregate Measurement of Support (AMS). The Agreement requires that developed countries should reduce the AMS by 20 per cent over a period of six years from the average level reached in the base period (1986–88). WTO members were under the obligation to enter their base-period AMS in their schedules, as well as the 'final bound commitment level' for the AMS.[365] Green subsidies are not included in AMS. *De minimis* supports (less than 5 per cent of the value of production for developed countries and 10 per cent for developing countries) are also excluded from inclusion in AMS. Under the Agreement, developed countries are required to reduce their export subsidy expenditure by 36 per cent in six years from the 1986–90 levels. The volume of subsidized imports is to be diminished by 21 per cent over six years. The rates of reduction for developing countries are 24 and 14 per cent respectively over 10 years. According to the Agreement, for products, which are not subject to export subsidy reduction commitments, no export subsidies can be granted.

The terms of accession of recent WTO members related to agricultural policies clearly reflect a new, more stringent ('WTO plus') approach which has been represented by countries (mainly the United State and members of the Cairns Group) whose aim is to gradually reach free trade in agricultural commodities.[366] After difficult negotiations, the principle of the 'most recent period for which data were available' was used for purposes of AMS calculations in the cases of Ecuador, Mongolia, Panama, Kyrgyz Republic, Latvia and Estonia. In the Bulgarian protocol of accession, because the most recent period was found not representative due to the United Nations embargo applied to Yugoslavia, a different period was taken as the base. Ecuador, Mongolia, the Kyrgyz Republic and Estonia have undertaken '*de minimis*' domestic support commitments because their domestic support measures fall either in the 'green box' or are below '*de minimis*' levels, either as a result of policy decisions or, mainly, lack of financial resources. The '*de minimis*' commitment means that for these countries product and non-product specific support must not exceed the 5 per cent level in the future. Latvia, however, negotiated a transitional period to 1 January 2003. During this period a special method, determined in Latvia's Protocol of Accession, will be used for the calculation of domestic support. It is interesting to note that for Bulgaria and Panama, reflecting a less stringent approach, maximum permitted levels of domestic support are provided by their schedules. For Bulgaria, for example, the AMS bound yearly commitment level between 1999 and 2001 has been specified as ECU520 million, while the base total AMS was ECU2513 million.

Ecuador, Mongolia, the Kyrgyz Republic, Latvia and Estonia have bound export subsidies at zero. The Bulgarian schedule, however, allows Bulgaria to grant export subsidies to the amount specified by quantity and value, for a number of products. The Bulgarian schedule does specify though some geographical areas to which the exports of certain subsidized products are excluded. Panama's schedule includes the commitment to eliminate its export subsidy by 31 December 1999.

Agricultural policies in Russia

Russia has vast land resources, which favour extensive farming.[367] General conditions for agriculture though are not favourable; soil in Russia is generally of low quality (with some exceptions in the southern part of the country) and the climate is predominantly continental with frequent droughts. The share of agriculture in the economy has declined since the beginning of the economic transition period, from 15.4 per cent in 1990 to 6.5 per cent in 1997, while the total working population in agriculture grew from 13 to 14 per cent over the same period and the volume of agricultural production fell by 36 per cent. This trend continued in 1998 and also in the first months of 1999. Production in March 1999 was 5 per cent below the level of March 1998. Cuts in consumer subsidies and a fall in real income resulted in a sharp decline in per capita food consumption. The terms of trade for agriculture worsened during most of these years: input prices, grew much faster than agricultural output prices and lack of liquidity, lack of capital and rising indebtedness were widespread. Access to credit was difficult as real interest rates were high. Changes in agricultural output have differed greatly across sub-sectors, commodities and regions. While production of large-scale agricultural enterprises halved, the output of household plots increased by 19 per cent between 1990 and 1996. Some regional administrations have prevented a drastic decline in agricultural production through state procurement and subsidies.

The production infrastructure of Soviet agriculture was dominated by large farms, – 'kolkhozes' and 'sovkhozes'. During the 1990s, the vast majority of large agricultural units have been reorganized, but only administratively. In practice, the reorganization has changed the institutional structure, management or production infrastructure of farms very little. Most farms have been converted into production co-operatives with fixed assets belonging to the collective under a form of share-based ownership. Land and non-land assets are owned collectively by the enterprises, and the enterprises are owned by shareholder employees or pensioners. Only about 10 per cent of large farms underwent more substantial restructuring. Uncertainty over land ownership rights has reduced interest in investments in agriculture, preventing the very much needed substantial restructuring of the sector. At the end of November 1997, 62 per cent of agricultural land was considered privately owned and the rest was still owned by the State or local municipalities. These figures, however, do not tell the whole story as the majority of the privately 'owned' land still takes the form of collectively shared ownership. Household plots occupy only 3 per cent of total agricultural land, divided among 16 million owners.

The aim of agricultural policies during the Soviet period was to ensure social stability and guarantee the supply of cheap food to the population. Consumer subsidies reached unsustainable levels in the 1980s. Policies used in agriculture distorted agricultural production to a huge extent. During the first years of economic transition, Russia did not have a clear concept of agricultural policy. Some *ad hoc* measures were introduced, but mainly the symptoms and not the roots of the problems were treated. The lack of budgetary sources was addressed by soft credits at the beginning of the period. According to the OECD Report 'The programme set for agriculture for the period 1996–2000 aims to increase Russian food self-sufficiency and to reduce dependence on food imports. The main tools envisaged to achieve these objectives are various input subsidies, and market intervention. These measures, if applied, would lead Russian agriculture back to a dependence on state intervention at great cost to consumers and taxpayers and to serious misallocation of resources.'

At the beginning of the transition period the use of trade policy instruments were determined by the undervalued rouble. At that time the aim of trade policy was to prevent a massive export of agro-food products, which was greatly facilitated by high world prices in terms of domestic currency. As the rouble started to appreciate, protectionist tendencies strengthened from 1993. At present, the tariff protection of the agricultural sector is not particularly strong compared with some OECD countries, with applied tariff rates ranging between 10 and 30 per cent. However, as the OECD Report underlines, the combination of tariffs 'with a multiplicity of legal acts issued at different levels... with complex and sometimes arbitrary modalities of customs valuation and with bureaucratic, time consuming and expensive certification, creates important trade barriers. Moreover, frequent changes to specific requirements and regulations... make trade policy untransparent for both domestic and foreign traders.'[368]

The economic transition process has also brought fundamental changes in the areas of price support and market regulation. The Soviet state procurement system was phased out but the state maintained some control on prices for agricultural products delivered to state reserves. At present, the main declared objective of state intervention is to stabilize agricultural prices on the domestic market. However, the market of agricultural products is far from coherent as there are unjustifiably large price differences between different regions due to lack of sufficient control at federal level and excessive intervention in market relations through subsidies (and otherwise), by regional authorities.

Since the 1960s, Russia has been a net food importer. In 1996, agri-food products represented 25 per cent of total imports and only 4 per cent of total exports. Since the beginning of the transition process there has been a striking shift in the product structure of Russian agri-food imports: imports of agricultural raw materials have fallen sharply while those of processed foods have increased. Since the economic collapse of 17 August 1998, due to the drastic depreciation of the rouble, total imports, including agri-food imports, have declined sharply. In the first three months of 1999, the value of Russian imports expressed in US$ declined by 48 per cent compared to the same period a year ago. Available information indicates that consumers have started to substitute food, alcohol, tobacco and other locally produced non-durables for better quality but more expensive Western imports.[369]

In the longer term, based on its comparative disadvantage in agriculture, Russia will probably remain a net importer of food and agricultural products. A policy aiming at self-sufficiency, let alone becoming a net food exporter, would distort the Russian economy and penalise other economic sectors in which Russia may have comparative advantages. The OECD has prepared detailed calculations to measure the assistance given to agricultural production in Russia. According to these figures, which indicate substantial fluctuations in support, the level of protection in Russia was lower than the OECD average in 1997.[370]

Accession negotiations between Russia and members of the Working Party face substantial obstacles in the area of agriculture. Russia's objective is to have an agriculture which can satisfy the basic needs of the country in the basic agricultural products and ensure Russia's food security. For this purpose Russia wants to secure a level of agricultural support and tariff protection which is comparable with the levels of WTO members and wants to ensure that domestic producers have the same competitive conditions as producers of the same products in other WTO members.

Areas of concern for a number of influential WTO members are centred around the following: Russia's highly complicated, bureaucratic and opaque trade regulations; trade relations with CIS countries which often involve fixed pricing and subsidies, and lack transparency; the strong power of the regions in agricultural matters which may endanger the implementation of trade concessions negotiated with the federal government; the identification of the base period for the estimation of the AMS. With regard to the base period concerning the AMS, Russia does not want to accept the 1993–95 period stating that it was a crisis period and therefore unrepresentative. Instead, Russia proposes that the 1989–91 period should be used which represents average, normal conditions. According to Russian calculations, the level of state support for Russian agriculture in that period was between US$80 and 90 billion.[371] Those who oppose the Russian position refer to the WTO practice of 'normally using the average of the most recent three year period'.[372]

Russia's accession negotiations are particularly difficult with regard to agricultural issues. Stakes are very high for both Russia and the members of the organization. Negotiations are aggrevated by Russia's continued economic troubles, the in-transparent federal structure and its frequently changing agriculture-related concepts and measures. The first problem, which should be overcome soon, is the selection of the base period to be used for the calculation of AMS, which would allow the country to table an offer on its agricultural commitments. Hopefully, both Russia and the members of the Working Party will take a flexible approach and find appropriate solutions which take account of Russia's specific situation in the transition period and the interest of the WTO system without using double standards for new members.

Trade-related intellectual property regime

International trade can be adversely affected if rules and practices to protect intellectual property rights vary widely from country to country. Furthermore, the inefficient enforcement of intellectual property rights can encourage trade in counterfeit and pirated products which damages the legitimate business interests of producers and other participants in business life who hold or have acquired these rights. Protection of intellectual property is also important for economic development as it provides an incentive to engage in costly long-term research and investment. The Agreement on Trade-Related Aspects of Intellectual Property Rights (TRIPS Agreement), negotiated in the Uruguay Round, is a comprehensive multilateral agreement which lays down minimum standards for the protection of intellectual property rights and basic procedures for their enforcement. The idea behind incorporating rules on the protection of intellectual property into the WTO system was that trade sanctions thereby could be made available to enforce the substantive provisions of the Agreement. The areas of intellectual property that are covered by the TRIPS Agreement are: copyright and related rights (that is, the rights of performers, producers of sound recordings and broadcasting organizations); trademarks including service marks; geographical indications; industrial designs; patents including the protection of new varieties of plants; the layout designs of integrated circuits; and undisclosed information including trade secrets and test data.

In respect of each of the main areas, the TRIPS Agreement sets out the minimum standards of protection to be provided by each member. It requires, as the main substantive obligation, that the major conventions of the World Intellectual Property Organization (WIPO), the Paris Convention for the Protection of Industrial Property (Paris Convention) and the Berne Convention for the Protection of Literary and Artistic Works (Berne Convention) must be complied with. Most of the substantive provisions of these conventions are incorporated by reference in the TRIPS Agreement, which also includes a number of additional obligations. The second main set of provisions lays down basic requirements on domestic procedures and remedies for the enforcement of intellectual property rights. The Agreement makes disputes between WTO Members with regard to TRIPS obligations subject to the WTO's dispute settlement process. Developed country members have had to comply with all of the provisions of the Agreement since 1 January 1996. According to Article 65:3 of the Agreement, for a country which is 'in the process of transformation from centrally-planned into a market, free-enterprise economy and which is undertaking structural reform of its intellectual property system and facing special problems in the preparation and implementation of intellectual property laws and regulations' the transition period is five years (1 January 2000). The transition period is also five years for developing countries. All members, however, had to comply with the national treatment and most-favoured-nation treatment as of 1 January 1996.

During all WTO accession negotiations members required acceding governments not only to apply fully all the provisions of the TRIPS Agreement but also to provide evidence of enforcement of rules that relate to the protection of intellectual property. All accession protocols concluded until now commit new members to full compliance with the Agreement upon the date of accession without recourse to a transitional period.

Since the beginning of its economic transition process, Russia has signed the most important international agreements on intellectual property and has passed laws which meet international standards. But Russia's business partners have frequently emphasized that mechanisms for the enforcement of intellectual property rights are insufficient and that piracy of intellectual property (for example broadcast and television signals, videos, video games and computer software) is of concern.[373] The Russian delegation declared in 1995 that an analysis of the TRIPS Agreement 'demonstrated no significant contradictions between the Russian Federation legislation on the protection of intellectual property and the said Agreement. Therefore, existing laws seem to be adequate for effective protection of intellectual property.'[374]

But members of the Working Party have specified many weaknesses in both the Russian legislation and the relevant practice, especially in the enforcement mechanism. They include: weak protection of intellectual property rights; the parallel existence of two different court systems (courts of justice and courts of arbitration) which can result in conflicting interpretation of laws; frequent delays in court cases; inadequate protection given to trademark owners; widespread piracy of intellectual property; lack of efficient procedures for suspending the entry of products into Russia which violate intellectual property rules; no sufficient criminal sanctions applied against counterfeiting and copyright piracy; lack of protection for retroactive copyright works and phonograms in accordance with the TRIPS Agreement; very high patent fees; Russia's failure to sign the Convention for the Protection of New Varieties of Plants; inadequate protection against the use of undisclosed information; non-uniformity of application of protection of intellectual property rights across all countries, due to some bilateral agreements.

Russia has clearly expressed that it would 'need a transitional period in order to fulfil certain obligations stipulated in the TRIPS Agreement.'[375] But in the light of the latest accession protocols, it is highly probable that Russia will also be asked to apply fully the provisions of the TRIPS Agreement by the date of its accession without recourse to any transitional period.[376]

Trade in services

The role of services has been constantly growing in recent decades. Currently, trade in services represents more than 20 per cent of all international trade. The United States and most other developed countries, which account for about 80 per cent of global exports of commercial services, insisted on the introduction of services to the agenda of the Uruguay Round. It was recognized that removing obstacles to international trade in services and improving predictability in this area could stimulate the world economy and could contribute to sustained economic growth. After long and difficult negotiations a General Agreement on Trade in Services (GATS) was adopted which applies the basic rules and principles on trade in goods to trade in services.

The system of services-related rights and obligations established by GATS can be divided into four parts: general principles and obligations;[377] annexes which deal with rules for specific sectors; specific commitments made by individual countries to provide access to their markets.[378] The fourth part includes a list indicating in which areas countries are temporarily not applying the most-favoured-nation principle. These commitments constitute an integral part of the Agreement. The Council for Trade in Services oversees the operation of GATS. At the end of the Uruguay Round, negotiations participants agreed to continue their negotiations in the areas of basic telecommunications, maritime transport, movement of natural persons and financial services. Negotiations on basic telecommunications and financial services were successfully finished in 1997, while those on maritime transport have been postponed to be resumed in the new services round which is expected to start in 2000. Negotiations on movement of natural persons were completed in July 1995, but with modest results.

Recent accession protocols indicate that the acceding countries have entered horizontal limitations in similar areas to original WTO members. These limitations include restrictions on real estate acquisition and ownership, and subsidies and restrictions on presence of natural persons. With regards to sector specific commitments, all new members have undertaken commitments across a large number of sectors, 'unlike some original Members in the Uruguay Round.'[379] (Broad coverage of sectors is common in case of high and middle-income countries; most new members, however, belong in the low-income group.) Sectoral commitments have generally minor or no limitations, but exclusions and m.f.n. exemptions are substantial except for Mongolia and the Kyrgyz Republic, the least developed among new members, which have no list of m.f.n. exemptions at all. All new members have undertaken commitments in professional services, business services, financial services, construction services and distribution services, but with different coverage and exclusions.[380]

In the Soviet Union low priority was given to services as they were considered an 'unproductive' sector of the national economy. Consequently, the development of services was neglected and this became a hindrance to productivity growth throughout the whole economy. Since the beginning of the economic transition process, services have become of growing importance in the country's economy, as a result of which the share of services in GDP increased from 42 per cent in 1993 to 55 per cent in 1998. Russia is a net importer of services. In 1997 imports (US$18.7 billion, 1.4 per cent of world imports) exceeded exports (1 per cent of world exports) by more than US$5 billion.

In the accession process Russia stressed that the regulatory framework governing services would, for some time, 'be subject to a process of frequent adaptation and improvement in light of experience and of progress made in building a national capacity to supply of services on a competitive basis.'[381] This uncertainty regarding the country's future services regime is one of the main reasons why Russia, until October 1999, had not been able to table its offer on specific commitments on services. Russia's present practices in this area are relatively liberal, but the authorities fear that their binding might create problems in future if, due to policy changes, more restrictions should be introduced.

Russia faces many specific challenges of a 'horizontal nature' in GATS-related accession negotiations. The movement of natural persons is one of them, which is a sensitive issue in almost all countries. Probably, Russia will also be expected to make similar horizontal commitments to those which other newly acceded countries have, especially those which facilitate intra-corporate transfer of highly skilled specialists. There are strong expectations that Russia will make market access and national treatment commitments for investments and commercial presence in most services sectors.[382] The lack of transparency regarding land ownership will also be an issue in services negotiations. The clarification of the situation in respect of ownership is of primary importance for foreign investments. Russia's federal system may also raise a number of problems as there are areas for which federal and regional authorities share jurisdiction or are otherwise required to work together, (for example matters related to the establishment of specific quotas for the employment of foreigners fall within the competence of the Russian Federal Migration Service that approves quotas but proposals for quotas are submitted by sub-federal authorities based on labour market needs).[383] Russia has concluded economic co-operation agreements with CIS countries. As these agreements are not compatible with Article V (Economic Integration) of the GATS, Russia will be obliged to negotiate m.f.n. exemptions for them. If these agreements were to be maintained for a longer period, Russia would be required to bring them into conformity with Article V of the GATS.

Some service sectors, such as financial and telecommunication services, play a decisive role in Russia's economic development. Rules impose special limitations on the activities of foreigners or dealings with foreign currencies in the banking sector. Banking operations in foreign currency, for example, can be conducted only by those credit organizations, which have currency licences from the Central Bank of Russia. Opening of a branch of a joint or foreign owned bank in Russia also requires a special licence. The share for foreign capital in the Russian banking system is limited to 12 per cent which is said to be incorporated in Russia's initial offer on services. The fear of a large influx of foreign banks has not been justified, as the participation of foreigners has remained well below the 12 per cent limit. There are also limitations in the insurance sector for foreigners. The weakness of the Russian banking sector, in which these restrictions play a role, became evident during the financial crises in 1998. As mentioned earlier, the banking sector, which consisted of about 2500 mostly small banks, did not provide the necessary support for the required economic restructuring. After 17 August 1998, a large number of banks went bankrupt, with US$15 billion in unmet obligations. But only very few of them actually went out of business.[384] The very important role of telecommunications in economic development is also widely recognized. Russia's outdated telecommunication sector urgently needs modernization which could be very difficult to achieve without it being substantially opened up to the world. (Russia's offer on services limits foreign equity participation in the telecommunication sector to 25 per cent.)

Russia has obvious difficulties in meeting all the requirements which have been and will be raised in the context of the GATS. The decisive task for Russia is to follow bilateral negotiations with WTO members on services and come to agreement with them.

Trade agreements

The latest accession protocols include the obligation for the acceding countries to observe the provisions of the WTO including Article XXIV of the GATT 1994 and Article V of the GATS in their participation in trade agreements, which include the fulfilment of notification, consultation and other requirements concerning free trade areas and customs unions. Article XXIV of the GATT 1994 allows the creation of free trade areas or customs unions on condition that trade barriers do not rise on average; all tariffs and other trade barriers are eliminated on substantially all trade within a reasonable length of time; and the agreements are notified to the WTO. The organization normally decides to establish a Working Party with a mandate to examine if these conditions laid down in Article XXIV are satisfied. Article V of the GATS contains similar provisions, allowing members to enter into agreements liberalizing trade in services, provided that such an agreement has substantial sectoral coverage; it provides for the absence or elimination of substantially all discrimination (defined as measures violating national treatment) either at the date of entry into force of that agreement or on the basis of a reasonable time frame; and it does not raise the overall level of barriers to trade in services in respect of third parties. The consistency of such agreements with the provisions of the GATS are examined in Working Parties established for this purpose.

As the Soviet Union stayed outside of the GATT, its trade relations with other countries were based on bilateral agreements. Russia, as a legal successor of the Soviet Union, inherited most of these agreements. At the beginning of the accession process Russia reported that it had international trade agreements with 138 countries and most of them (126) included a most-favoured-nation clause.[385] In 1992 and

1993, Russia concluded bilateral free trade agreements with CIS countries which account for about one fourth of Russia's foreign trade. The fundamental principle included in all free trade agreements is not to apply tariff and non-tariff restrictions. During a transition period, annual protocols define the goods that are excluded from free trade treatment. Originally, these goods included those, which were subject to export duties, (later, export tariffs were abolished, then, in respect of some goods, reintroduced). Under the free trade agreements, VAT is not collected on imports originating from CIS countries. The amount of excise tax is reduced by the amount of excise tax already paid in the country of origin.

On 24 September 1993, CIS countries signed an Economic Union Treaty. The treaty provides for a phased creation of a common economic space with free movement of goods, services, capital and labour. This is to be achieved through a step-by-step establishment of a free trade zone, a customs union, a common market for goods, services, capital and labour, and a monetary union.

In April 1994, the CIS states signed a multilateral agreement on a free trade area. The agreement expresses the intention of the parties to provide conditions for free trade in goods over the entire territory of CIS states. It envisages a half-year period, from the entry into force of the agreement, for a transition from a bilateral free trade regime to a multilateral system, with a common list of goods and services to be excluded from free trade treatment during the transition period.

In January 1995, Russia and Belarus signed an intergovernmental Agreement on a Customs Union. Kazakstan and the Kyrgyz Republic joined the Agreement in January 1995 and March 1996. Tajikistan joined the Agreement as the fifth member in November 1998. The signatories have accepted the Customs Union goals, operating principles, mechanisms and stages of its formation, the distribution of customs duties, taxes and charges, the rules applicable to the imposition of temporary restrictions and customs control. Until the middle of 1999, no common import customs tariffs have been established for the purposes of the Customs Union. At present, trade in goods between the signatories of the Customs Union Agreement is carried out under free trade conditions, without any restrictions or exemptions.

CIS countries have signed hundreds of agreements related to different sectors of their mutual economic relationship.[386] In March

1995, the meeting of the CIS Intergovernmental Council agreed to set up a Common Agrarian Market of the CIS Member States. In October 1997, the Agreement for a Common Agricultural Market among eight CIS countries was signed, which is subject to ratification. The Agreement specifies stages for creating a common agricultural market, without indicating deadlines.

The liberal terms under which the Kyrgyz Republic acceded to the WTO has caused some friction between the Kyrgyz Republic and the other signatories of the Customs Union Agreement. The source of the problems is that tariffs bound by the Kyrgyz Republic are substantially lower than tariffs applied by Russia and other signatories of the Customs Union Agreement. (Liberal Kyrgyz commitments in some services sectors, for example banking, may also lead to some conflicts with other members of the Agreement.) This fact will certainly make the establishment of a common external tariff of the Customs Union very difficult. The head of the Russian delegations at the WTO accession negotiations stated reproachfully that, 'The Kyrgyz commitments to allow foreign goods and services in to their market are not compatible with the idea of a union with other participants. But nobody will prohibit Kyrgyzstan to join WTO. It is her sovereign right to pursue such policy.'[387] Evidently, the Kyrgyz Republic accession to the WTO under their own terms was considered not only an economic but also a political question. The acceptance of the country's WTO accession terms by WTO members may have been considered an important contributions to the formation of the country's own trade regime through which its independence has been strengthened.

Russia and Belarus had already developed a very close co-operation in political and economic matters during the early years of their independence. In May 1997, the two countries signed a Union Pact which laid down some basic principles of a union between them. At the end of 1998, the two presidents signed a declaration of further unification of Russia and Belarus, a treaty on equal rights of citizens and an agreement on the creation of equal conditions for economic entities. In April 1999, the two presidents signed 11 further documents concerning the union between their countries. The documents signed include agreements on the formation of a single customs space and unified border policy. The presidents agreed that a Treaty of Unification of Russia and Belarus would be worked out before the middle of 1999. However, according to a Russian statement made at the end of June 1999, the process of reunification will take a long time, 'probably up to several years'.[388]

Russia concluded a Partnership and Co-operation Agreement with the European Union, which entered into force in December 1997. This Agreement provides a forum for political dialogue between Russia and the EU and includes trade- and investment-related provisions, including a m.f.n clause, without establishing a preferential relationship. The preamble recognizes that Russia is no longer a state trading country, it is a transition economy, (as a result, Russia is no longer on the list of non-market economies regularly published by the EU and therefore, in anti-dumping procedures against Russian exporters, the EU no longer applies the specific and burdensome rules which are used in respect of non-market economies).

In the preamble of the Agreement it is indicated that one of its aims is 'to create the necessary conditions for the future establishment of a free trade area between the European Community and the Russian Federation'. The parties to the Agreement will examine when circumstances will allow the commencement of negotiations on the establishment of a free trade area. The Agreement reconfirms the removal of all quotas and other quantitative restrictions on Russian exports to the EU, with such exceptions as textiles and steel. The Agreement provides for some preferences in favour of EU service providers.

The Agreement on Trade Relations between Russia and the United States took effect in 1992. Based on this Agreement, the US accords m.f.n. status to Russia regarding customs duties and other charges, methods of payments etc. The m.f.n status, however, is temporary, subject to renewal under the terms of the Trade Act of 1994 (Jackson–Vanik amendment). At present, Russia is still on the list of countries against which the United States might be obliged to invoke the non-application clause (Article XIII) of the WTO Agreement. The invocation of Article XIII by the United States would prevent the establishment of WTO relationship between the two countries. The United States similarly to the EU, Japan and most other developed countries, provides GSP treatment to most products imported from Russia.

7
Outlook for Russia's WTO Accession

Analysis included in earlier chapters has demonstrated that, after eight years of inconsistent economic reforms, Russia is still very far from a smoothly functioning market economy. It has turned out that expectations for a quick transformation of the country into a modern market economy belonged to the realm of utopias. A successful economic transition needs further efforts from Russia and co-operation, understanding and support from the rest of the world, but first of all a great deal of patience.

Obviously, there is a close link between Russia's transformation into a functioning market economy and its accession to the WTO. The latter presupposes the former. It would be, however, a serious mistake to take a fundamentalist approach in accession matters. Among the WTO's present members many are also far from an ideal market economy. Still, the GATT/WTO system has found the ways and means to integrate them without making irreparable damage to the system. A similar solution should also be found in case of Russia.

To what extent can Russia be considered WTO compatible?

From the point of view of WTO compatibility, Russia shows a contradictory picture. The examination of Russia's trade system has revealed that there are only few areas where the country's trade regime is in conflict with WTO rules. There are, however, very substantial problems in the implementation of trade-related (and other) rules. There are frequent and unpredictable changes in regulations. Lack of stability and transparency is a major source of concern for

Russian and foreign businesspeople. Wide discretionary powers granted to the administration lead to arbitrary practices and facilitate corruption, which is the rule rather than the exception. Organized crime has become a major economic factor that competes with the weak Russian state and has taken over some state functions. Difficulties in implementation are due to the traditionally weak legal system and the poorly developed institutions. Another area of concern is the constant fight between the executive power and the parliament, which expresses the lack of consensus in Russian society concerning some basic questions of political and economic reforms. These problems are aggrevated by Russia's sophisticated federal system that makes compliance with federal laws and decisions of the federal authorities questionable.

There are some specific institutions where Russia needs some more time to bring all rules and practices into harmony with WTO requirements. In the area of technical barriers to trade as well as sanitary and phytosanitary measures Russia, after long decades of total isolation, understandably requires time to introduce standards, regulations and certification systems which are based on international norms. Problems in the sphere of state trading are related to some conceptual problems regarding the participation of the state in trade and economic matters. As it was indicted, even the establishment of the list of state trading enterprises constituted a problem. Russian privatization has not been finished which explains the important role Russian state-owned foreign trade enterprises still play in exports and imports. Lack of transparency and poorly developed regulations in government procurement are related to the complete absence of traditions in this field, and general legal and institutional weaknesses. Russia's trade-related intellectual property regime is not far from compatibility with WTO rules, at least at the level of regulations. However, enforcement of rules leaves much to be desired. Therefore, complaints are particularly frequent in this area.

The most serious problems, which have been identified during the Russian accession process, are related to the lack of consistent basic economic strategies and policies. Controversies about Russia's tariff offer indicate the lack of a clear concept regarding some main trade policy objectives and the future of the basic economic sectors. The beginning of the reform process was marked by economic and trade liberalism. This was greatly facilitated by a deeply undervalued rouble and the liberal orientation of the executive. Later, as different lobbies could better organize their ranks, protectionist tendencies strengthened. After the Russian crisis in August 1998, the government made frequent declarations about the need to develop the 'real sector' of the economy. However, the depreciation of the domestic currency and the resulting collapse of imports prevented the introduction of substantial new import barriers. As a result of the contradictory developments, a 'wait and see' policy has strengthened. Russian negotiators hesitate to undertake liberal tariff commitments in many industrial sectors because of fears from the damaging effects of increased import competition. These concerns in respect of certain specific sectors may be justified, as some newly privatized Russian infant industries may deserve a provisional tariff protection. However, it should be kept in mind that all so-called 'provisional' protective measures which are not taken in the context of a clear long term commitment for the liberalization are counterproductive. For Russia, economic isolationism represents more danger than sustainable economic liberalism.

As for commitments in agriculture, where Russia, concerning most products, clearly does not have comparative advantages, a protectionist tariff policy, or excessive support to the sector would put in danger the success of the reforms. Such a policy would distort the economy and would penalise other sectors, which may have competitive advantages. At present, Russia's objective is to have an agriculture, which satisfies the domestic needs in the basic agricultural products and ensures the country's food security. These policies, however, seem to be based on political considerations rather than on economic logic. The debate between Russia and members of the Working Party on the base period concerning the AMS reflects that difference in approaches. Hopefully, Russia will avoid following the example of Western Europe that has developed overprotected and over-supported agriculture to the detriment of other economic sectors. Finding a healthy compromise between economic and general policy objectives could also contribute to reaching a satisfactory solution in the issue of the base period.

Russia, tabled its initial services offer only in October 1999. This again reflects some conceptual contradictions and confusion. Russia is in the process of developing her own services sector and wishes to give a substantial degree of protection for it. The quick development of the country's services sector has created many new work places and attracted substantial foreign investments but the liberalization of the country's services market is still subject to significant opposition. The view is widespread that Russian insurers, banks and other sectors are not yet ready for competition against foreigners. There are exaggerated fears that foreigners might take over some services sectors, which would be considered as a dangerous development.[389] The question remains, however, that without the participation of foreigners what other sources are available for the much-needed modernization of the Russian services sectors.

WTO membership under what conditions?

The former socialist countries, especially Poland and Romania, but also Hungary acceded to the GATT under special, non-standard conditions. The reason for the creation of this special group within the contracting parties was that their trade and economic regime was not compatible with the basic market-oriented rules and principles of the GATT. The accession of the socialist countries involved a substantive deviation from the basic GATT philosophy, but the danger of causing systemic damage to the multilateral trade system was acceptable in exchange for the political advantages expected from the introduction of some new elements of division into the monolithic socialist camp. After the demise of the Soviet Empire and the collapse of centrally planned socialist economies, these political considerations did not exist any more and the trade regimes of most transition economies, thanks to market economy reforms, ceased to be incompatible with WTO requirements. Therefore, there are no incentives any more to tolerate any major deviation from the spirit and letter of the globalizing trade order. Therefore, also in case of transition economies, including Russia, accession to the WTO is required to take place under normal terms.

This new situation, however, does not mean that accession conditions should not take account of special situations that are related to the transitional nature of the economy. Commitments that ignore existing macroeconomic instabilities, structural rigidities, poorly developed economic, legal and social institutions, can not be sustainable. For Russia, time is needed until a social consensus is formed which can provide solid foundations for the development of WTO consistent economic strategies and implementation mechanisms. If these special conditions are ignored, the most that can be achieved is WTO compatibility, which while it exists only on paper will not stand the proof of implementation.

There is a broad consensus among economists about the economic benefits of trade liberalization.[390] There can be no doubts that liberalism will also contribute to Russia's economic development. But in the context of Russia's WTO accession the big question is how to stage the introduction of a consistent, WTO conform liberal trade regime. As indicated in earlier chapters, if liberal economic reforms are introduced in total disregard of a country's possibilities, the result can be counterproductive. This is also true for steps of trade liberalization. The degree and speed of liberalization expected from Russia in the context of WTO accession should take into account both the social and the private costs of adjustments. The observation is also valid for Russia that 'adjustment costs are one of the key factors that create resistance to trade liberalization.'[391] Without efficient government measures to mitigate the adverse effects of income losses and ease the difficulties of the adjustment period, popular support for trade liberalization and market economy reforms in general will further diminish. In developed countries social safety nets which include unemployment insurance, social assistance, and adjustment assistance programmes have already been established.[392] In Russia, however, these programmes are either nonexistent or very rudimentary. If the hardships of the population are to be further increased due to drastic liberalization resulting from WTO accession, the already small support given to economic reforms will fade away. As a consequence, it may facilitate the take-over of power by extremist forces in Russia, with unforeseeable consequences for the world. Therefore, the objective should be to draft accession conditions, which include substantial, but sustainable liberalization, both in trade in goods and services. That might include transitionary periods with pre-established deadlines and close WTO monitoring.

The length of time needed for the completion of the accession process is still an open question. What is sure is that Russia needs some time to form its new economic strategy, which would correct the mistakes which led to the August 1998 crises. In the context of a new economic strategy it will be easier to take decisions in such outstanding accession-related matters as narrowing the gap between applied and bound rates, the level of protection to be given to agriculture, or liberalization in trade in services. Hopefully, Russia and other countries, which might not join the WTO before the next round of trade negotiations, can participate in the round as observers. This would provide additional information for Russia for the necessary changes required to be made in its trade regime.

The stakes of the Russian WTO accession are high. Other, smaller CIS countries are much more reliant on the multilateral trade system due to their size, product compositions of their trade and the small bargaining power they represent. Examples of a number of transition economies which have recently joined the WTO have demonstrated that they are willing to except even 'WTO plus' obligations to get early membership. Russia, however, may opt for staying outside the WTO and turn towards economic isolation if accession conditions are not satisfactory. That would be a big economic loss for the globalizing world economy and would entail substantial political risks. The world would be less safe with a noncooperating Russia.

Notes

Chapter 1

1 Article 28, Suggested Charter for an International Trade Organization of the United Nations, *U.S. Department of State*, Pub. No. 2598, Com. Policy Ser. No. 93 (1946).

2 For further details see: J.M. van Brabant (1989) and W.L. Richter (1988).

3 For a description of Soviet attitudes towards the GATT see: Richter (1988) pp.487–99.

4 The need for a new approach to the GATT was also reflected by the unexpected announcement in 1955 by centrally planned economies that they were in favour of multilateralism and non- discrimination, Kostecki (1979), note 13, p.5.

5 Czechoslovakia, similarly to other socialist countries, did not enjoy a normal GATT treatment during its non-market economy period. In 1951 the US Congress decided that the US administration could no longer grant m.f.n. treatment to communist countries, including Czechoslovakia. The United States wanted to revoke the m.f.n. treatment for Czechoslovakia on the basis of Article XXXV of the GATT. Czechoslovakia contested this US legal position. The contracting parties, after a long debate charged by heavy political elements, authorized both parties to the dispute to suspend their obligations.The United States unilaterally suspended GATT benefits for Czechoslovakia, which reciprocated this step accordingly. Some other market economies, for example the European Community, imposed discriminatory quantitative restrictions on imports from Czechoslovakia which were not consistent with Article XIII of the GATT. Similar treatment was given to Cuba.

6 Cuba was also an original member. Yugoslavia became an observer in 1950, Poland and Romania in 1957, Hungary in 1966 and Bulgaria in 1967.

7 Report of the Working Party on the Accession of Poland, *GATT Basic Instrument and Selected Documents (BISD)*, 15th Supplement, p.110.

8 Report of the Working party on the Accession of Romania, *GATT, BISD*, 15th Supplement, p.94.

9 In the 1927 Latvian–Soviet commercial agreement, in exchange for the m.f.n. treatment, the Soviet Union undertook the purchase of Latvian goods to the value of Rouble 15.4 million. This agreement was followed by some others containing similar quantitative import commitments. For details see M. Domke and J. Hazard (1958), p.56.

10 'Protocol for the Accession of Poland', Annex B. *GATT, BISD* 15th Supplement, p.52.

11 'Protocol for the Accession of Romania', Annex B, *GATT, BISD*, 18th Supplement, p.10.

12 *GATT, BISD* 20th Supplement, p.34.

13 The effectiveness of the Hungarian tariffs was the subject of serious discussions. The EC opposed Hungary's request that tariff concessions be accepted as entrance fee, while the US delegation supported the Hungarian suggestion. The Note of the GATT Secretariat 'The Operation of the Hungarian Tariff and its Role in Hungary's Foreign Trade' did not answer all the sensitive questions, but it certainly reflected the special role the Hungarian tariffs played after the introduction of inconsistent market economy reforms in 1968. The Note stated: 'At present, it can be fairly said, however, that the functions of the tariff and the rate of customs duty are somewhat different than those in the majority of the developed GATT countries. This is particularly true of many investment goods which, while not produced in Hungary, are subject to high rates of duty.' GATT document, Spec (70)83, 23 September 1970.

14 It is generally recognized that the acceptance of Hungarian tariff concessions as an entrance fee was also attributable to the negotiating skills of Janos Nyerges, Hungary's representative at the accession negotiations. Mr Nyerges had a strong vision about Hungary's place in the GATT as a country enjoying equal rights with other contracting parties. He rejected proposals that Hungary should also accept some forms of quantitative commitment. In July 1969, in his statement introducing Hungary's application for accession to the GATT he stated: 'When asking for full membership I should like to stress that Hungary does not wish to be treated in any different manner from any of the contracting parties.' GATT document, L/3238, 1 August 1969. See also L.A.Haus (1992) pp.43–52.

15 'Protocol for the Accession of Hungary', *GATT, BISD* 20th Supplement pp.3–8.

16 In informal conversations it was frequently noted that neither the Polish nor the Romanian protocols did address properly CMEA-related issues. The Polish Protocol remained silent about the CMEA, while the Romanian quantitative import commitment squarely discriminated against trade with the country's socialist partners. As Hungarian economic reforms suffered a setback from 1972, the question became very sensitive. In view of the fact that the Hungarian protocol allowed for Hungary to maintain its existing trade regulations regarding the fourteen socialist countries listed in the Annex to the protocol, the Hungarian negotiating team could argue against the domestic GATT opposition that the Hungarian protocol was very positive concerning the country's trade relations with its socialists partners and it even gave some international legitimacy to internal socialist, mainly CMEA trade.

17 The terms of the protocols of accession of the three countries on the issues of discriminatory quantitative restrictions and selective safeguards were substantially different.

18   In 1971, the Polish import commitment was changed to an increase in the total value of Polish imports from the contracting parties by '7 per cent per annum aggregated and compounded over multi-year periods'. *GATT, BISD*, 18th Supplement, p.200.

19   See for example the Reports of the Romanian Working Party on its first and sixth (last) meeting, *GATT, BISD*, 20th Supplement, pp.217–24; *GATT, BISD*, 35th Supplement, pp.337–46.

20   'Report of the Hungarian Working Party', *GATT, BISD*, 20th Supplement, p.35.

21   E.R. Patterson (1986) p.192.

22   L.A. Haus (1992) p.61.

23   For a more detailed criticism see: E.R. Patterson (1986) pp.188–189 and K.C. Kennedy (1987) pp.31–2.

24   M. Kostecki (1979) p.14.

25   For more details see L.A. Haus, (1992) pp.11–24.

26   The first Trade Policy Review Report of the GATT Secretariat on Hungary noted that before the reforms of 1989/90 '. . . price related border measures had a modest impact on Hungarian trade flows. While customs and tariffs were applied to imports settled in convertible currencies, their main impact was to generate Government revenue. Trade with market economies was largely regulated by comprehensive non-automatic import licensing, trade-related trade monopolies, and other instruments, including a sophisticated system of formal and informal State and Party interventions in enterprise decisions affecting foreign trade.' GATT (1991) Vol.I., p.12.

27   For the decisive role of political considerations see: L.A. Haus (1991).

28   Debates were especially heated at the sessions of the Hungarian Working Party. Hungary attacked the EC for not lifting these restrictions. The US, CANADA, Japan and a number of other countries always supported Hungary in this issue. GATT Documents L/4228, L/4633, L/5303/, L/5635, and L/5977.

29   It was noted: 'The establishment of Part V would not only have a serious disintegrating effect on the whole system, but it would contradict the realities of life and it would prove to be irreconcilable with the tendency of differentiation of the economic and trade system of countries included in the group in question.' J. Martonyi (1989) p.277.

30   Czechoslovakia ceased to exist on 31 December 1992, its successor states, the Czech Republic and the Slovak Republic had to apply for contracting party status in the GATT. In April 1993, both countries became contracting parties under the usual standards of membership, without any special conditions. Slovenia also became contracting party at the end of 1994. It joined the WTO in 1995.

31   Patterson suggests a number of elements to be adopted as guidelines for future entrance fees. E.R. Patterson (1986). A similar approach was also taken by K.C. Kennedy (1987) W.L. Richter (1988) and J.M. van Brabant (1989).

32   E.R. Patterson (1986) p.203.

Chapter 2

33 'K Peresmotry Obschego Soglasheniya o Tarifakh i Torgovle' (Towards a Review of the GATT), *Vneshnyaya Torgovlya* (Foreign Trade) No.10, 5 (1955) quoted by W.L. Richter (1988) note 67.

34 M. Kostecki (1979) p.14.

35 According to the Tokyo Ministerial Declaration, the participation in the Round was 'open to any other government, through a notification to the Director-General'. It was also stated 'that negotiations will involve the active participation of as many countries as possible.'

36 At the end of 1982, the author also participated in one of such consultations with a leading Soviet GATT expert. The questions put to the Hungarian officials suggested that the Soviet Union, at that time, did not reject the idea of full participation in the GATT and was studying the eventual legislative changes which could be required from the Soviet Union, if it wanted to get contracting party status on tariff basis. The Soviet expert suggested that the Hungarian GATT accession model was considered the most successful one by Soviet specialists. The impression of the author at that time was that Soviet experts were not aware of all the economic and political implications of an eventual accession on tariff basis. (It seemed that the Soviet authorities were ready to introduce a customs tariff, however, there was no willingness to change other related elements of the economic system, for example the price system or the currency and exchange rate regulations.)

37 In the GATT, unlike UNCTAD and most other UN organizations, there was no regional group system. Centrally planned economies with contracting party status did not have any institutionalized form for co-ordinating national positions. At different GATT fora they all expressed national positions based on their economic and trade interests. Co-ordinating positions would had been particularly difficult between Hungary, which joined the GATT on tariff basis, and other centrally planned economies which paid for their contracting party status with quantitative import commitments. In the case of the Soviet Union's eventual participation in the GATT, the pressure for expressing co-ordinated positions in politically sensitive issues would have been an aspect to reckon with. For this reason, Central and Eastern European contracting parties were really not enthusiastic about the prospects of a Soviet presence in the GATT in any form. Of course, they were not in a position to represent this view openly.

38 W.L. Richter (1988) p.479.

39 'Soviet Union Seeking Observer Status, May Want to Participate in New Round', *International Trade Reporter*, (BNA) No.13, 397 (26 March 1986).

40 The Soviet Union applied only for the right to participate in the Uruguay Round and not for a formal observer status. V. Ognivtsev and S. Chernyshev (1989) p.29.

41 J. Croome (1995) p.35.

42 M. Lavigne (1989) p.10.

43 '... Western officials were concerned that Soviet participation may lead to an "UNCTADization" of GATT...', L. Haus (1991) p.172.
44 '... denial of Observer status to the Soviet Union was short-sighted.', W.L. Richter (1988) p.523; '...the stance adopted in 1986 was regrettably short-sighted, to say the least.' J.M. van Brabant (1989) p.75.
45 Gorbachev quoted President Bush saying: 'We used to oppose Soviet membership of this organization.... We have now reviewed our position: we suggest granting the Soviet Union observer status in GATT. However, the member states need some time.' M. Gorbachev (1995) p.660. See also L.A. Haus (1992) pp.96–8.
46 *Financial Times*, 5 December 1990.
47 GATT Document, L/6654, 12 March 1990.
48 L.A. Haus (1992) pp.94–5; *Financial Times*, 4 January 1990; *Reuter*, 3 January 1990.
49 GATT Document, C/M/241, 8 June 1990.
50 In line with the practice that, in political matters the GATT followed the decisions taken by the United Nations, contracting parties took note that the observer status conferred to the former USSR would be continued by the Russian Federation. GATT Document, C/M/254, 10 March 1992.
51 GATT Document, L/7243, 14 June 1993.
52 *Reuter*, 11 June 1993.
53 Statement by Mr S. Glaziev, Minister for the External Economic Relations of the Russian Federation at the meeting of the GATT Council of Representatives, 16 June 1993. *Press Bulletin*, Permanent Mission of the Russian Federation (Geneva), Number 152 (2587), 16 June 1993.
54 GATT Document, C/M/264, 14 July 1993.
55 Terms of reference of the Russian Working Party: 'To examine the application of the Government of the Russian Federation to accede to the General Agreement under Article XXXIIII, and to submit to the Council recommendations which may include a draft Protocol of Accession.' The Chairman of the Working Party became W. Rossier, Ambassador, Permanent Representative of Switzerland to the GATT. GATT Documents, L/7259 and Rev.1, 8 July and 24 November 1993.
56 WTO Document, WT/ACC/RUS/9, 23 April 1996, p.26.
57 Document of the Preparatory Committee for the WTO, PC/W/26, 20 December 1994. Article XII (Accession) of the WTO Agreement states the following:

1. Any State or separate customs territory possessing full autonomy in the conduct of its external commercial relations and of the other matters provided for in this Agreement and the Multilateral Trade Agreements may accede to this Agreement, on terms to be agreed between it and the WTO. Such accession shall apply to this Agreement and the Multilateral Trade Agreements annexed thereto.
2. Decisions on accession shall be taken by the Ministerial Conference. The Ministerial Conference shall approve the agreement on the

terms of accession by a two-thirds majority of the Members of the WTO.

3. Accession to a Plurilateral Trade Agreement shall be governed by the provisions of that Agreement.

Chapter 3

58 M.I. Goldman (1996) p.8.
59 A. Åslund (1995) p.29.
60 W. Andreff (1989) 71–102; P. Naray (1989) pp.95–6.
61 A. Åslund (1995) p.38; A. Åslund (1997) p.15; J.R. Blasi, M. Kroumova and D. Kruse (1997) pp.20–1.
62 A. Åslund (1995) p.29.
63 All together 12 economic reform plans were proposed to Gorbachev, but none of them were accepted by him. M.I. Goldman (1996) pp.68–77.
64 According to reports, Gorbachev remained unwilling to split the Communist Party into a conservative Communist and a social-democratic block under his own leadership, although, it happened a little later. R.B. Ahdieh (1997) pp.32–3.
65 The adopted laws in the area of freedoms included the Law on the Press and Other Mass Media (June 1990); the Law on Freedom of Conscience and Religious Organizations (October 1990); the Law on Public Associations and the Declaration of Individual Rights and Freedoms (September 1991).
66 R.B. Ahdieh, (1997) p.31.
67 It was noted that Gorbachev began to rule as a monarch, with decrees becoming increasingly arbitrary and controversial. R. Ahdieh (1997) p.35.
68 R. Ahdieh (1997) p.21.
69 J.R. Blasi *et al.* . . . (1997) pp.24–5.
70 M.I. Goldman (1996) p.89.
71 A. Åslund (1995) p.64 and M.I. Goldman (1996) p.90.
72 In 1992, Gaidar became deputy prime minister and from 15 June 1992 he was the acting prime minister.
73 Foreign advisers for the Russian government, mainly Americans, included G. Allison, A. Åslund, R. Blackwill, M. Dabrowski, S. Fischer and J. Sachs.
74 In the first stage, most prices were to be deregulated and foreign economic relations were to be partially liberalized. Proposal was made on the introduction of foreign exchange actions and partial liberalization of export and import transactions, without convertibility for the rouble and without a unified exchange rate. The next stage of the reform, the introduction of a convertible Russian rouble, was to be implemented after eight to nine months. M. Dabrowski in A. Åslund (1997) p.46.
75 A. Åslund (1995) p.65; M. Dabrowski (1997) p.46–8.
76 For a description of the measures taken see: ECE (1992) pp.138–46.
77 It was estimated that controlled prices still covered about 30 per cent of GDP at the beginning of 1995. OECD (1995) p.27.
78 ECE (1992) p.143.

79   ECE (1993) p.159.
80   OECD (1995) p.87.
81   OECD (1995) p.27.
82   OECD (1995) p.28.
83   A. Åslund (1995) p.141.
84   A. Åslund, (1995) p.142.
85   A. Åslund, (1995) p.142–145.
86   This section is based on data and analysis published by different editions of the 'Economic Survey of Europe', prepared by the Secretariat of the Economic Commission for Europe.
87   ECE (1993) p.161.
88   ECE (1993) p.161.
89   OECD (1995) p.96–7.
90   ECE (1993) p.183.
91   The objective was to collect taxes to the value of 40–42 per cent of net material product. ECE (1992) p.121.
92   For a detailed analysis of the Russian banking sector see: OECD (1997) pp.78–111.
93   In Russia, the proportion of enterprizes with less than 250 employees was 53 per cent of the total number of enterprizes. These enterprizes employed 8.5 per cent of the manufacturing workforce. These proportions in the US were 98 per cent and 27 per cent respectively. OECD (1995) p.88–90.
94   ECE (1993) p.173.
95   ECE (1992) p.145.
96   A. Åslund (1995) p.146.
97   ECE (1993) p.162.
98   The name of the ministry was frequently changed. In early 1998, it became Ministry of Industry and Trade, from October 1998 it was the Ministry of Trade.
99   Russian domestic oil prices sometimes reached only 3 per cent of world prices.
100 For details see: O.D. Davydov (1998) p.25.
101 P. Aven (1997) p.65.
102 A. Åslund (1995) p.151.
103 P. Aven (1997) p.62.
104 If Russia had fixed the exchange rate at the end of 1991, it would have caused an inflation rate of almost 2000 per cent until December 1993. The IMF was criticized for not providing any stabilization fund before the stabilization of the exchange rate. As mentioned, after the stabilization the fund was not needed any more A. Åslund (1995) p.182.
105 It was reported that, due to the inefficient banking and financial system, there was a notable gap between when hard currency was surrendered by an exporter and when actually the rouble equivalent of the surrendered hard currency ended up in the exporter's account. P. Aven (1997) p.64.
106 OECD (1995) p.16.

107 A. Åslund (1995) p.109.
108 It is interesting to note that the IMF was in favour of maintaining the rouble zone 'and threatened that countries that launched their own currencies would not receive any IMF support.' A. Åslund p.110. J.D. Sachs states that 'the IMF asserted that the non-Russian republics were not ready to manage their own currencies. In saying this, the IMF failed to recognize that the continued use of the Soviet rouble as a common currency virtually guaranteed highly inflationary policies in the non-Russian republics, and therefore the stabilization during 1992.' (1997) p.128.
109 On 24 July, CBR announced that all pre-1993 bank notes would be withdrawn from circulation. Economic units were instructed to transfer all their pre-1993 bank notes to banks by 26 July, and citizens could also convert up to rouble 35 000 into new roubles until 7 August. In view of the protest by the public, the rouble amount was increased to 100 000 and the deadline extended until the end of August.
110 OECD (1995) p.16.
111 According to a survey of 132 cities taken on 25 February 1992, 3 per cent of cities had a shortage of eggs, 4.5 per cent of milk and 9 per cent of potatoes. In more than 50 per cent of cities, acute shortages were observed in the case of wheat flour, macaroni, rice, rye bread, cheese, milk powder, tinned fish, and sweets. Dabrowski, (1997) p.48.
112 The CBR 'central rate' remained at 80 per cent since end May 1992, while the lending rate of major commercial banks varied around 90–120 per cent, much below the rate of inflation which was running at about 900–1000 per cent annually. ECE (1993) p.165.
113 The rouble was sharply devalued in January 1992. The exchange rate stayed at the level of 110/US$ until June. It collapsed, however, in the second half of the year, falling to 440/US$ in December 1992.
114 The stock of credit jumped by 76 per cent during September–October alone. ECE (1993) p.165.
115 ECE (1993) p.165.
116 For more details about changes in life conditions see: A. Illarionov, *et al.* (1997) pp.137–58.
117 ECE (1993) p.168.
118 ECE (1994) p.123.
119 The development of central bank interest rates between 1991 and 1993 was the following: 1991: 8 per cent; 1992: 1 January, 20 per cent; 7 April, 50 per cent; 23 May, 80 per cent. 1993: 30 March, 100 per cent; 2 June, 110 per cent; 22 June, 120 per cent; 29 June, 140 per cent; 15 July, 170 per cent; 1 October, 200 per cent; 15 October, 210 per cent. ECE (1994) p.124.
120 Total import subsidies were reduced from 17.5 per cent to 4 per cent of GDP between 1992 and 1993. A. Åslund (1995) p.196.
121 ECE (1994) p.125.
122 A. Åslund (1995) p.199.

123 By December 1994, the share of these credits in total bank credits declined below 20 per cent, while at the end of 1992, it was 59 per cent. OECD (1995) pp.33–4.

124 In 1993, total tax revenue amounted to 9.1 per cent of GDP, while in 1994 and 1995 it declined to 8.8 per cent of GDP. OECD (1995) p.34.

125 In the USSR, government budget revenues, similarly to a number of developed market economies, were close to 50 per cent in 1990. Between 1992 and 1995, the share of budget revenues in GDP fluctuated between 25 and 30 per cent, which represented a lower level than in the case of Australia or the United States. Similar tendencies could be observed in respect of total revenues of consolidated government budgets as a share of GDP. The figure for Russia in 1994 and 1995 was 28.2 and 26.1 per cent, while for Central European countries they were close to 50 per cent. V. Popov (1996) pp.22–3.

126 OECD (1995) p.35.

127 OECD (1995) pp.35–6.

128 V. Popov (1996) p.24.

129 OECD (1995) pp.36–7.

130 A. Åslund (1995) p.215. Of course, the lack of appropriate business morals in Russia was a well-known fact. It was a serious mistake that reformers or their foreign advisers did not take it into account when shaping economic policies and institutions. It is similarly misleading to state that arrears 'exist in all market economies, where trade credits are a standard feature.' Ibid p.209. Obviously, in a market economy trade credits take a totally different form, they are part of normal business life and have almost nothing in common with arrears in transition economies.

131 V. Popov (1996) p.25.

132 OECD (1995) pp.96–7.

133 P. Bonne and B. Fedorov (1998) p.171.

134 A. Åslund (1995) pp.226–7, M. Boycko (1996) pp.72–3.

135 R. Blasi *et al.* (1997) p.37.

136 One hundred and fifty million vouchers were distributed for a small fee to all Russian citizens. Almost everybody (98 per cent) picked up and invested the vouchers.

137 The privatization programme included the following three options: Option 1: offered employees (workers and managers) 25 per cent of non-voting shares in their firm. In addition, workers could buy 10 per cent of shares at 30 per cent discount of the January 1992 book value under preferential payments conditions. Option 2: workers and managers were allowed to buy, against cash or vouchers without preferential payments conditions, 51 per cent of voting shares at 1.7 times the book value of the assets at 1 July 1992. (In the light of the high inflation, the price offered was extremely low.) Option 3: it applied only to medium-sized enterprizes, allowing the managers to buy a maximum of 40 per cent of shares at very low prices subject to a commitment of ensuring the solvency and the employment of the enterprise for at least one year.

138 OECD (1995) p.77.
139 M. Boycko (1996) p.111.
140 J.R. Blasi *et al.*, (1997) p.54.
141 Management had a majority in about 5 per cent of the enterprises in 1996. J.R. Blasi *et al.* (1997) pp.63–6.
142 OECD (1997) p.138.
143 OECD (1997) pp.140–2.
144 M.I. Goldman (1997) p.45.
145 One example of the gross abuses was that the management simply refused to register the ownership of a new owner. J.R. Blasi *et al.* (1997) p.90.
146 J.R. Blasi *et al.* (1997) pp.89–92.
147 As a result of CBR interventions, by the end of 1996, foreign exchange reserves declined to one-and-a-half months of imports. OECD (1997) p.48.
148 OECD, for example, projected a 3 per cent growth , 10 per cent inflation and a stable rouble for 1998. OECD (1997) p.75.
149 A. Elder wrote, in April 1998, in the foreword to his book, which included proposals on how to make money on Russian financial markets, the following: 'Nobody can tell how high the economy will rise, but Russia has a democracy, an emerging system of modern law, a huge market, and vast natural, financial, and human wealth. An investment boom is unavoidable, like spring and summer after a long winter.... Not only Russians, but Westerners, too, can profit from these changes. Very rarely in life can you profit, have fun, and do good at the same time. That time in Russia is now!' (1998) ix.
150 M. Camdessus, Managing Director of the IMF, declared already in April 1996 that 'In many respects, 1995 marked a turning point in Russia's reform effort.' 'IMF, Stabilization and Reform', address by M. Camdessus, at the US–Russia Business Council, Washington, DC, 1 April 1996. At the beginning of 1998, S. Fischer stated that 'Six years after the start of the Russian economic reform process, much has been achieved and the continued progress of the economy towards economic normalization is not in doubt. IMF,' 'The Russian Economy at the Start of 1998', S. Fischer, 9 January 1998.
151 The share of loss-making industrial eneterprizes amounted to 43 per cent. OECD (1997) p.115.
152 In 1996, the share of total broad money (broad money is domestic currency plus foreign currency deposits) in Russia reached only 14.1 per cent of GDP. Corresponding figures for Hungary and Poland were 45 and 35.6 per cent, respectively. In the Baltic countries these values ranged between 17.4 and 23.7 per cent. ECE (1997) p.72.
153 By the end of 1997, foreigners held about 33 per cent of GKOs and OFZs. By mid-1998, their share exceeded 50 per cent. EBRD (1998) p.13.
154 ECE (1997) p.72.

155 'A drive around most provincial cities provides graphic evidence of wages paid in kind. For example, the highway to Yaroslav runs through the textile district around Ivanovo. Along the road are stalls staffed by workers from these factories trying to sell the towels, sheets, shirts, and other cotton goods they have been paid in lieu of wages. In other cities workers have been paid in toilet paper, tires, shoes, trucks, manure, condoms, brassieres, tombstones, and coffins. Even when cash is paid it may not come in the form of wages but in a more byzantine fashion. For example, since interest earned on savings accounts was tax-free until July 1998, many employers set up savings accounts in their workers' names so the workers could collect tax-free interest rather than the equivalent amount in taxable wages.' Goldman (1998) p.324.

156 ECE (1998/1) p.70.

157 In 1996, less than 17 per cent of the enterprises were deemed to comply with their tax obligations in full and on time. In the same year, 26 tax inspectors were reportedly killed, many injured. Staff morale was affected by wage arrears. The appearance of fake tax police officers confiscating property or levying pseudo fines also negatively influenced taxpayer compliance. OECD (1997) p.59.

158 EBRD (1997) p.121.

159 ECE (1998/3) pp.37–8.

160 OECD (1997) p.117.

161 According to OECD calculations, in 1996, the share of money surrogates in regional budgets was 60.3 per cent and in local budgets 42.9 per cent. OECD (1997) p.181.

162 K. Loukine (1998) p.627.

163 R. Wintrobe (1998) p.603.

164 C. Gaddy and B.W. Ickes (1998/a) pp.1–4.

165 C. Gaddy and B.W. Ickes (1998/b) p.60.

166 Legal acts at federal level include: Federal Constitution, Federal Constitutional Laws, Federal laws and Codes, Duma or Federation Council decrees, Presidential decrees, Presidential orders, Cabinet decrees, Cabinet orders and Administrative rules.

167 OECD (1997) p.220.

168 P.H. Rubin (1997) p.42.

169 P.H. Rubin (1997) p.33.

170 P.H. Rubin (1997) p.31.

171 OECD (1997) p.136.

172 P.H. Rubin (1997) pp.37–43. Inflows of foreign direct investments in Russia between 1993 and 1998 in billion US$: 1993: 1.2; 1994: 0.6; 1995: 2.0; 1996: 2.5; 1997: 6.2; 1998: 2.2. *UNCTAD*, press release, 2 June 1999.

173 J.M. Kramer (1998) p.330.

174 *Transition*, August 1997 p.20.

175 EBRD (1997) p.37.

176 M.B. Katyshev (1998) pp.3–4.

177 M.B. Katyshev (1998) pp.4–6.
178 P. Rutland and N. Kogan, (1998) p.26.
179 M. Newcity (1997) p.41.
180 The frequency of homicide in Russia (and Estonia) is extremely high in international comparison, above 20 per 100 000 persons, and has doubled since 1990. Imprisonment rates in Russia per 100 000 population are the highest in Europe (including the United States, Canada and CIS). ECE (1999) pp.223–37.
181 J.M. Kramer (1998) p.331.
182 M. Newcity, (1997) p.42.
183 M. Newcity, p.43.
184 V.D. Mazaev (1998) p.4.
185 Russian Organized Crime, *The Economist*, 28 August 1999, pp.15–17.
186 For examples see: P.H. Rubin (1997) pp.50–1.
187 P.H. Rubin (1997) p.51.
188 F.J. Cilluffo and R. Johnston (1997) p.59.
189 M. Galeotti (1998) p.421.
190 M. Galeotti (1998) p.418.
191 OECD (1995) p.50.
192 O. von Luchterhandt (1998) pp.12–22.
193 OECD (1995) p.50.
194 N. Rubin (1998) pp.545–66.
195 *International Herald Tribune*, 24 September 1998.
196 For more details about the different regions see OECD (1995) pp.52–7.
197 Revenue assignment of the provinces was: 100 per cent of personal income, corporate income, land and property taxes, 50 per cent of excise taxes and 60 per cent of natural resource taxes. OECD (1995) p.59.
198 OECD (1995) p.62.
199 OECD (1997) pp.186–97.
200 Foreign investors pulled out of Russia about US$2 billion in January 1998. *International Herald Tribune*, 31 January–1 February 1998.
201 *International Herald Tribune*, 1 June 1998.
202 ECE (1998/3) p.33.
203 ECE (1998/3) p.33.
204 ECE (1998/3) p.33.
205 The main reason behind the decline of Russian exports was the fall in oil prices. In 1997, the annual average price for crude petroleum was US$ 19.19 per barrel. By December 1998, the price of crude oil had fallen to US$10.41. Oil prices started to climb from March 1999 and by summer, they exceeded US$20 per barrel. UNCTAD, *Monthly Commodity Price Bulletin*, different numbers.
206 IMF, *Public Information Notice*, No. 99/67, 2 August 1999, p.2.
207 In the first three months of 1999 imports declined by 48 per cent. ECE (1999/2) p.44.
208 IMF, *Public Information Notice*, No. 99/67, 2 August 1999, p.2.

209   Statement of the government of the Russian Federation and Central
       Bank of Russia on Economic Policies, 13 July 1999, pp.1–19, IMF website
       (www.imf.org).
210   IMF, *Press Release*, No. 99/35, 28 July 1999, p.1.

Chapter 4

211   'The Russian reformers tended to refer to Poland as the most relevant
       model . . .', A. Åslund (1995) p.83; 'Russia has also proved that it is not
       essentially different from other countries.' ibid. p.312. 'After three years
       of Poland's reforms and one year of Russia's reforms, I remain absolutely
       convinced in the potential for successful economic reforms throughout
       the region. Events have disproved the idea of a "homo sovieticus"
       spoiled by decades of communism.' J. Sachs (1994) p.xiii. IMF orthodoxy
       (macroeconomic discipline, microeconomic deregulation and liberaliza-
       tion, and outward orientation) was also applied to Russia without the
       necessary adaptation to the Russian special situation.
212   M. Newcity (1997) p.48.
213   M. Newcity (1997) p.48.
214   M. Newcity (1997) p.47.
215   T.C. Owen (1997) p.24. Similar thoughts were expressed also by Newcity:
       'The models for the Russian monarchy were the Byzantine emperor and
       the Mongol khan, both of which modelled an absolute, centralized
       monarchy as compared with the more limited monarchies that charac-
       terized Western Europe. This model of absolute authoritarian power has
       persisted in Russia from medieval time to the present.' (1997) p.50.
216   M. Newcity (1997) p.50.
217   The weak institutional foundations of Russia's market economy can be
       demonstrated by some historical facts. For example: in 1892, in the
       European part of Russia, over 90 per cent of agricultural land occupied
       by peasants was in communal ownership. In Russian peasant communes
       most affairs were regulated by customary practices, which were generally
       regarded as having greater significance than legal rules. M. Newcity
       (1997) pp.50–1.
218   EBRD 1998 (and earlier) average transition indicators clearly prove this
       point. The first nine places in the list are occupied by countries scoring
       an average of 3 points or above, which belong to the Western socio-
       cultural area (Hungary, Poland, the Czech Republic, Estonia, Slovakia,
       Slovenia, Latvia, Croatia and Lithuania). They are followed by South-
       eastern European and CIS countries with scores substantially below 3
       points. EBRD (1998) p.29.
219   I. Bestuzhev-Lada (1998) p.30.
220   A. Åslund (1997) p.16.
221   A. Åslund (1997) p.17.
222   R. Layard, Foreword to J. Sachs (1994) p.x.
223   A. Åslund (1997) p.16.

224 Poland's slow privatization and gradual institutional reforms put a question mark to the qualification that the country was really following the 'big bang' approach.

225 A. Åslund (1995) p.267. Of course, in 1999, at the time of writing this book, there is no need to convince the reader who followed the right path of privatization, Russia or Hungary. But the correctness of Hungarian privatization methods, based mainly on sales against cash and involvement of foreigners, were evident much earlier, already at the time of Russian mass privatization. Foreign investors, who had no preconceptions, made quick decisions and acted accordingly, heavily investing in 'unprofitable and parasitical' Hungarian state-owned enterprises and avoided Russia. Later, other countries followed the Hungarian example. EBRD (1998) p.30.

226 R. Frydman, A. Rapaczynsky, and J. Turkewitz (1998) p.52.

227 In 1998, the highest average of transition indicators was achieved by Hungary. EBRD (1998) pp.22–38.

228 According to a study prepared by the WTO and the UNCTAD, about 10 per cent of all Quad country tariffs are still above 12 per cent *ad valorem* with some tariff peaks reaching 350 per cent or more, and the majority of peaks being somewhere between 12 and 30 per cent. The sectors concerned include textiles and clothing, footwear, leather and travel goods, fish, processed foodstuffs and agricultural products. *WTO Press Release*, Press/122, 19 February 1999.

229 It is obvious that in almost all European developed countries the agricultural sector, due to very substantial state support, is oversized. Those who wish to downsize the agricultural sector are 'right', those who are against it, are 'wrong'. Nevertheless, despite the crystal-clear textbook type case, nobody is suggesting that downsizing should take place immediately and without compensation for those who tend to be the losers, just because at a certain point in their life, normally due to circumstances beyond their control, they happen to be farmers (steel or textile workers, coal miners and so on).

230 ECE (1993) pp.7–8.

231 ECE (1993) p.10.

232 In Russia, in October 1992, only five per cent were satisfied with the economic situation; 16 per cent with their standard of living and 10 per cent with the political situation. ECE (1993) p.11.

233 S.A. Vasiliev (1997) p.29.

234 A. Åslund (1995) p.9.

235 A. Åslund (1997) p.14.

236 R. Kozul-Wright and P. Rayment (1997) p.551. The answer of shock therapists to this charge was that 'Current decision-makers should not avoid policies simply because they are reminiscent of the Bolsheviks.' A. Åslund (1997) p.16.

237 In the context of executive power, it is worthwhile to refer to the conclusion of a study made on transitions economies which states that

'stronger executives are associated with less economic reform and that under stopgap constitutions the consequences of strong executive powers are even worse for economic reform. Stable constitutions that place constraints on executive, and hence state, power appears to have a positive effect on the process of economic reform, even in this still early stage of post-communist transitions.' J.S. Hellman (1997) p.73.

238   S. Medvedev (1997) p.80.

239   A. Åslund (1997) p.20. The Russian minister of foreign trade has drawn similar conclusions: '. . . any obstacle to economic activity, especially one which assumes the existence of a discretionary choice, will be circumvented in Russia, and therefore, this country has to be more liberal than any other.' P. Aven (1997) p.65.

240   Some macroeconomic indices improved but at the same time millions suffered because of declining standards of living, the backlog in wages, or increasing criminality.

241   ECE (1993) p.16.

242   R. Kozul-Wright and P. Rayment (1997) p.645.

243   ECE (1998/3) p.34; EBRD (1998) p.17.

Chapter 5

244   The multilateral agreements are included in Annexes 1–3 to the WTO Agreement. They are the following: Annex 1A: General Agreement on Tariffs and Trade 1994 it will be referred to as 'GATT 1994', it is legally distinct from the GATT, dated 30 October 1947, which will be referred to as 'GATT 1947'; Agreement on Agriculture; Agreement on the Application of Sanitary and Phytosanitary Measures; Agreement on Textiles and Clothing; Agreement on Technical Barriers to Trade; Agreement on Trade-Related Investment Measures; Agreement on Implementation of Article VI of the General Agreement on Tariffs and Trade 1994; Agreement on Implementation of Article VII of the General Agreement on Tariffs and Trade 1994; Agreement on Preshipment Inspection; Agreement on Rules of Origin; Agreement on Import Licensing Procedures; Agreement on Subsidies and Countervailing Measures; Agreement on Safeguards. Annex 1B: General Agreement on Trade in Services; Annex 1C: Agreement on Trade-Related Aspects of Intellectual Property Rights; Annex 2: Understanding on Rules and Procedures Governing the Settlement of Disputes; Annex 3: Trade Policy Review Mechanism. The texts of the main Uruguay Round Agreements and decisions are included in GATT (1994).

245   The plurilateral trade agreements originally included the Agreement on Trade in Civil Aircraft, the Agreement on Government Procurement, the International Dairy Agreement and the International Bovine Meat Agreement. In September 1997 the signatories of the International Dairy Agreement and the International Bovine Meat Agreement decided to terminate these agreements as of 1 January 1998.

246 Michalopoulos, 1998a, pp.1–4.
247 *Press Bulletin*, Permanent Mission of the Russian Federation (Geneva), Number 152(2587), 16 June 1993.
248 Davydov (1998) pp.14–17.
249 President Yeltsin declared: 'Russia will enter the world economy not as a raw-material appendix but as a developed industrialized country and an equal partner.' *Press Bulletin*, Permanent Mission of the Russian Federation (Geneva), Number 642 (3076), 12 May 1998.
250 *Press Bulletin*, Permanent Mission of the Russian Federation (Geneva), Number 634 (3068), 18 March 1998.
251 *The St Petersburg Times*, 10–17 February 1997.
252 G. Gabunia, at that time head of the Russian WTO team, was quoted to state: 'We want to join but not at any cost.' *Press Bulletin*, Permanent Mission of the Russian Federation (Geneva), Number 590 (3024), 3 July 1997. See also the comments made by A. Chubais following the Denver G8 summit meeting in June 1997. *Radio Free Europe/Radio Liberty*, Internet web-site (23 June 1997).
253 WTO Document, WT/MIN(98)/ST/59.
254 L. Sabelnikov (1996) pp.346–7.
255 *Press Bulletin*, Permanent Mission of the Russian Federation (Geneva), Special Issue, 29 October 1998.
256 'On measures for socio-economic stabilization', *Press Bulletin*, Permanent Mission of the Russian Federation (Geneva), Number 669 (3102), 18 November 1998.
257 *Press Bulletin*, Permanent Mission of the Russian Federation (Geneva), Number 671 (3104), 2 December 1998.
258 President's annual State-of-the Nation address to the Federal Assembly, *Press Bulletin*, Permanent Mission of the Russian Federation (Geneva), Special Issue, 30 March 1999.
259 Statement of the government of the Russian Federation and Central Bank of Russia on Economic Politics, 13 July 1999, IMF internet website.
260 To illustrate the importance of political considerations it is enough to recall that China's negotiations for resumption of its status in the GATT started 13 years ago. The Working Party on Algeria's accession was established in 1987, but the substantive work has not yet been started. Accession of Bulgaria to the GATT/WTO took about ten years.
261 For the issues raised by the US business community see, for example, the letter of 5 December 1997 of the US Council for International Business to the US Trade Representative internet website), or the communication of the American Business Alliance for the Transition Economies, The US Chamber of Commerce, updated on 6 February 1998 (internet website).
262 Europe, Russia and the World trading system, speech given by Sir Leon Britten, Vice-President of the European Commission to the Duma of the Russian Federation, 17 June 1997. EU External Relations (Internet website).

263   Singapore Ministerial Declaration, paragraph 7, WTO Document, WT/ MIN(96)DEC, 18 December 1996.

264   WTO Document, WT/MIN(98)/DEC/1, 25 May 1998.

265   Until July 1999 the following countries became WTO Members. Conditions of membership are set out in WTO documents (and addenda) as indicated: Ecuador (January 1996, WT/L/77 and Corr.1), Bulgaria (December 1996, WT/ACC/BGR/5 and Corr.1), Mongolia (January 1997, WT/ACC/MNG/9 and Corr.1), Panama (September 1997, WT/ ACC/PAN/19 and Corr.1), the Kyrgyz Republic (December 1998, WT/ ACC/KGZ/26 and Corr.1) and Latvia (February 1999, WT/ACC/LVA/32). Accession negotiations have also been finished with Estonia, but its membership is subject to ratification.

266   For details see: WTO Document, WT/GC/M/32, 9 February 1999. The European Communities laid down its position on accession matters in a separate document which included proposals on the acceleration of the accession procedure in general, but with special emphasis on least developed countries ('fast track procedure'). The paper also includes a suggestion on the participation of acceding countries in the forthcoming new round of trade negotiations. WTO Document, WT/GC/W/153, 8 March 1999.

267   *Press Bulletin*, Permanent Mission of the Russian Federation (Geneva), Number 479 (2913). 10 June 1998.

268   Joint Statement on US–Russia Economic Initiative, *Daily Bulletin of the U.S. Mission to the United Nations* (Geneva), 24 March 1997.

269   Britten, Trade Commissioner of the European Commission, was also quoted saying that it was 'a mistake' for the Americans and the Russians to put a date on projected membership. *Radio Free Europe/Radio Liberty*, 23 June 1997 (internet website). The allegation was also made that 'President Clinton agreed to support Russian WTO membership by late 1998 as one of several steps apparently aimed at easing Russian heartburn over expansion of the North Atlantic Treaty Organization.' *The Journal of Commerce*, 20 August 1997.

270   This was the comment by Ms Barshefsky on President Yeltsin's proposal that Russia be admitted to the WTO in 1998. *International Herald Tribune*, 21 May 1998. See also similar comments by US Undersecretary of Commerce for International Trade, D. Aron. *Reuters*, 1 April 1998.

271   These countries/customs territories were the following: Albania, Algeria, Andorra, Armenia, Azerbaijan, Belarus, Cambodia, People's Republic of China, Croatia, Estonia, Georgia, Jordan, Kazakhstan, Lao People's Democratic Republic, Lithuania, Former Yugoslav Republic of Macedonia, Moldova, Nepal, Oman, Sultanate of, Russian Federation, Samoa, Saudi Arabia, Seychelles, Sudan, Chinese Taipei, Tonga, Ukraine, Uzbekistan, Vanuatu and Vietnam.

272   WTO Document, WT/AC/1,4 and 7; *Focus*, WTO Newsletter, No.34, October 1998.

273 For a detailed description of the accession procedures and the followed
     practice regarding transition economy applicants see: C. Michalopoulos,
     (1998/a) pp.2–5; P. Milthorp (1997) pp.217–18.
274 O.D. Davydov (1998) p.75.
275 C. Michalopoulos (1998/a) p.17.
276 C. Michalopoulos (1998/a) pp.18–19.
277 C. Michalopoulos (1998/a) pp.20–3.

Chapter 6

278 For details see the appropriate sections of the Trade Policy Review Report
     on Hungary, GATT (1991).
279 The reporting period is one year for the Kyrgyz Republic, Latvia and
     Estonia, 18 months for Bulgaria and two years for Mongolia.
280 Recently, deputy minister of the Russian Ministry of Economics declared:
     '. . . tariffs must protect domestic production to the maximum extent for
     the whole period of reorganization. . . .The Russian market can be
     opened only after the period of complicated economic restructuring is
     over, stable growth achieved and the budget stabilized.' *Press Bulletin*,
     Permanent Mission of the Russian Federation (Geneva), Number 703
     (3136), 14 July 1999.
281 Article III:9 of the GATT 1994 includes the following provision: 'The
     contracting parties recognize that internal maximum price control mea-
     sures, even though conforming to the other provisions of this Article,
     can have effects prejudicial to the interests of contracting parties supply-
     ing imported products. Accordingly, contracting parties applying such
     measures shall take account of the interests of exporting contracting
     parties with a view to avoiding to the fullest practicable extent such
     prejudicial effects.'
282 Prices for products and services of natural monopolies (transportation
     of oil and gas through pipelines, transmission of electrical power and
     heat, carriage by rail, services of transport terminals, ports and airports,
     services of public postal and electrical communication systems) are sub-
     ject to price controls by federal authorities. Prices of natural gas, nuclear
     fuel cycle products, defence products and precious metals are also
     administratively controlled. Local governments regulate prices for cap-
     ital goods and services which include, *inter alia*, energy products sold
     to the population, passenger and luggage transportation, rents and con-
     sumer services, water supply and sewerage, mark-us on pharmaceuticals,
     medical and other goods, and certain telecommunication services.
     Sometimes, local authorities put a ceiling on the growth of prices for
     food products or medicines, prices of which are not regulated by the state
     through subsidies. For more details see: WTO Document, WT/ACC/RUS/
     4, 1 November 1995. In respect of retail prices of food items, the com-
     ment was made that 'the regional governments were given the power to
     regulate retail prices without any federal co-ordination of such a policy.'

OECD (1998) p.113. In the agricultural sector, the 1992 reforms abolished the centrally administered food prices and compulsory deliveries to the state. Between 1992 and 1997, in some cases, fixed prices (grain) or guaranteed minimum prices (grains, oilseeds, milk, meat products) were used if the products were purchased for federal reserves. In 1997, a Federal Law (State Regulation of Agro-food Production), with the objective to stabilize prices on the domestic market, introduced the concept of guaranteed prices at which the state authorities have to buy agricultural production if the average market prices are lower than the guaranteed price. OECD (1998) pp.111–14. The coverage of administrative price controls has been gradually reduced, though after the economic collapse in August 1998 regional price controls have became more frequent.

283 For the interpretaion of this obligation see: Understanding on the Interpretation of Article XXIV of the General Agreement on Tariffs and Trade 1994, which was adopted in the Uruguay Round.

284 Paragraph 28 of the Report of the Working Party on the Accession of the Kyrgyz Republic.

285 See paragraph 30 of the Working Party Reports of the two countries.

286 US Commercial Relations with the Russian Federation, the United States Chamber of Commerce, International Division, internet website, last updated 6 February 1998.

287 According to the example cited, regional authorities prevented the establishment of branches of Russian and foreign banks, even if the matter was in theory dealt with by federal law. WTO Document, WT/ACC/RUS/ 14, 1 November 1995, pp.99–100.

288 WTO Document, WT/ACC/RUS/Add.1, 30 May 1996, p.3.

289 WTO Document WT/ACC/7, 10 March 1999, includes a detailed analysis on the tariff negotiations with the six new members.

290 In case of ceiling bindings all, or a large part of tariff lines are bound at a specified level, normally well above the applied tariff rates.

291 The post Uruguay Round scope of bindings for some other groups, expressed in percentage, are as follows: Central and Eastern Europe: 97; Latin America: 100; Africa: 90; Asia: 70.

292 Mongolia and Panama bound most of the items in headnote, at the level of 20 and 30 per cent.

293 The same average for Mongolia: 20 per cent; Bulgaria: 12.6 per cent; Panama: 11.5 per cent; and Latvia: 9.3 per cent. Ecuador, the Kyrgyz Republic and Latvia have bound all non-agricultural items individually. Mongolia, Bulgaria and Panama have bound only some of their non-agricultural tariffs individually, the remaining items have been bound in a headnote. (Those items are bound in a headnote, on which no specific requests were made by WTO members.)

294 Some examples on simple average bound rates negotiated at the Uruguay Round in two main product groups (agriculture and manufactures) expressed in percentage terms: Argentina: 22.64 and 31.39; Brazil: 100

and 100; Chile: 25 and 25; Egypt: 91.92 and 32.78; the Philippines: 35.04 and 25.98; Thailand: 34.12 and 27.48; and Tunisia: 114.50 and 48.84. Source: WTO, IDB, quoted by C. Michalopoulos (1998/b), table 3.

295 Information provided by the European Union Sectoral and Trade Barriers Database, internet website.

296 See for example: 'Russia's WTO Application Advances', *International Economic Review*, January/February 1998 pp.3–5; US Council for International Business Recommendations on Russia's Accession to the WTO, 5 December 1997, internet website; US Commercial Relations with the Russian Federation, updated 6 February 1998, internet website.

297 Government Resolution No.1347, October 1997.

298 'Russia: Acting Trade Minister Defends Import Strategy for WTO' Moscow, 18 May 1998, *Radio Free Europe/Radio Liberty*, internet website.

299 O.G. Davydov (1998) p.75; 'Reasonable Protectionism', *Expert*, 7 September 1998.

300 Press Bulletin, Permanent Mission of the Russian Federation, Number 703 (3136), 14 July 1999.

301 D. Tarr (1999) pp.15–25.

302 D. Tarr (1999) pp.10–11.

303 As Russia is joining the WTO under developed country conditions, these provisions are included in Article XII of the WTO 1994 and Article XII of the GATS. Article XII:1 of the GATS has the following particular provision which applies to developing countries and transition economies: 'It is recognized that particular pressures on the balance-of-payments of Member in the process of economic development or economic transition may necessitate the use of restrictions to ensure, *inter alia*, the maintenance of a level of financial reserves adequate for the implementation of its programme of economic development or economic transition.'

304 WTO Document, WT/ACC/RUS/2, 2 June 1995, pp.95–6.

305 VAT and excises are collected if the amount paid in the country of origin is below the amount to be paid in Russia.

306 Russia provided information on import licensing in WTO Document WT/ACC/RUSS/10, 23 April 1996.

307 WTO Document, WT/ACC/RUS/9, p.110, 23 April 1996.

308 Decision Regarding Cases where Customs Administrations Have Reasons to Doubt the Truth or Accuracy of the Declared Value.

309 'Russia's WTO Application Advances', *International Economic Review*, January/February 1998 p.5.

310 For some of the critical comments see: Old Russian Customs, *The Economist*, 8 May 1999, p.79; P. Davies (1998), L. Savchenko and J. Boiarsky (1998), 'Russian trade, New Customs', *The Economist*, 25 July 1998, pp.76–7. In this article, the head of the State Customs Service admitted that 'The level of corruption is very high . . . in the past two months 1,500 officers have been relieved of their posts; many more will go.'

311 Article 18:1 of the Agreement includes the following provision: 'No specific action against dumping of exports from another Member can

be taken except in accordance with the provisions of GATT 1994, as interpreted by this Agreement.' It is clear that taking anti-dumping actions is not subjected to the existence of national anti-dumping legislation. Such actions can be taken on condition that they are in accordance with the provisions of the GATT 1994.

312 Federal Law No.62–FZ.

313 Government Resolution No.783, 17 July 1998.

314 Paragraph 2 of the Understanding on the Balance-of-Payments Provisions of the GATT 1994.

315 Paragraph 3 of the Understanding on the Balance-of-Payments Provisions of the GATT 1994.

316 Government Resolution No.413, 11 April 1996.

317 *Press Bulletin*, Permanent Mission of the Russian Federation (Geneva), Number 679 (3112), 28 January 1999.

318 In case the price of the Urals blend goes below US$9.8 a barrel, exports are duty free for 30 days. If the average monthly price ranges between US$9.8 and 12.3 for a barrel, the export tax will be lowered to Euro 2.5. *Press Bulletin*, Permanent Mission of the Russian Federation (Geneva), Number 705 (3138), 28 July 1999.

319 'Statement of the Government of the Russian Federation and Central Bank of Russia on Economic Policies', 13 July 1999, pp.9–10. IMF website.

320 O.D. Davydov (1998) pp.22–4.

321 WTO Document, WT/ACC/RUS/9, pp.19–20, 23 April 1996.

322 Industrial policy can be considered to encompass all actions undertaken by governments that have an effect on the structure of production in an economy. B. Hoekman and M. Kostecki (1995) p.105.

323 M. Landesmann (1993) p.2.

324 WTO Document, WT/ACC/RUSS/9/Add.1, pp.6–8, 30 May 1996.

325 ECE (1995) p.52.

326 WTO Document, WT/ACC/RUSS/4, pp.37–9, 1 November 1995.

327 See for example: the 'President's Annual State-of-the Nation Address to the Federal Assembly', *Press Bulletin*, Permanent Mission of the Russian Federation Geneva), Special Issue, 30 March 1999.

328 Article 27 of the Agreement provides a transition period of eight years to developing countries to bring their subsidy practice into conformity with the requirements of the Agreement.

329 For a detailed description of the rules see: ITC (1995) pp.145–57.

330 WTO Document, WT/ACC/7, pp.6–7, 10 March 1999.

331 In 1997, Russia provided export subsidies to two engineering companies in the form of soft loans. This subsidy was terminated in 1998.

332 In 1997, the total amount of subsidies was US$14.4 billion. WTO Document, WT/ACC/RUS/ADD.1/Rev.1, 9 December 1997.

333 WTO Documents WT/ACC/RUSS/22, 24 November 1997 and Add.1, 2 December 1997.

334 'Russia's WTO Application Advances', *International Economic Review*, January/February 1998, p.4. See also the similar comment made by the US

Council for International Business, 5 December 1997, USCIB website. Comments of EU companies are summarized in the EU Sectoral and Trade Barriers Database, EU website.
335 Some of the relevant WTO documents which include detailed information on the problems in this area: WT/ACC/RUSS/2, pp.135–8, 2 June 1995; WT/ACC/RUSS/9, pp.56–61, 23 April 1996; WT/ACC/RUSS/23, pp.3–45, 2 December 1997.
336 For an illustrative list of 13 TRIMs see: ITC (1995), Box 24, p.208. Out of 13 TRIMs listed, only five are covered by the TRIMs Agreement.
337 In 1998, for example, inflows of foreign direct investment reached US$2.5 billion in the Czech Republic and US$5.1 billion in Poland. ECE (1999/2) p.79.
338 'eubusiness' website.
339 For details see: ECE (1998/3) pp.135–49.
340 *Press Bulletin*, Permanent Mission of the Russian Federation (Geneva), Number 695 (3128), p.9, 19 May 1999.
341 UNCTAD Document, UNCTAD/ITCD/TSB/3 pp.33–4, 15 April 1998.
342 WTO Document, WT/ACC/RUSS/5/Add.1, 21 November 1997.
343 In the area of privatization of municipality's owned property, the automobile industry and bank loans, other examples of WTO inconsistent TRIMs have been identified. J. Bergsman, H.G. Broadman, and V. Drebentsov (1999) pp.70–1.
344 WTO Document, WT/ACC/RUS/13, p.23, 23 August 1996.
345 For example, in the 1970s and 1980s, Hungary, Poland and Yugoslavia reported that they did not have state trading enterprises.
346 Article VIII:1 of the GATS provides that 'Each Member shall ensure that any monopoly supplier of a service in its territory does not, in the supply of the monopoly service in the relevant market, act in a manner inconsistent with that Member's obligations under Article II and specific commitments.'
347 WTO Document, WT/ACC/RUS/4, pp.154–5, 1 November 1995.
348 The list included nine joint companies: RAO Gazprom (natural gas); MES (crude oil); Ferreign (pharmaceutical); Alfa-Eco (crude oil, sugar); Menatep-Impex (crude oil, sugar); Raznoimport (nonferrous metals); Roscontract (crude oil, oil products, agriculture products); Nafta-Moscow (crude oil); Rosinvestneft (crude oil) and the state enterprise Machinoimport (crude oil). WTO Document, WT/ACC/RUS/9, 23 April 1996.
349 The difficulties in qualifying the activity of exporters for state needs in terms of Article XVII of the GATT 1994 is a further example of the uncertainty of the criteria of state trading. The Russian delegation referring to 'exports for state needs' declared: '... to a certain extent, companies conducting this trade might be covered by the working definition of 'State trading enterprizes'. WTO Document, WT/ACC/RUSS/9/Add.1, pp.4–5, 30 May 1996.
350 WTO Document, WT/ACC/RUS/18, p.1, 11 March 1997.
351 WTO Document, WT/ACC/RUSS/4, p.152, 1 November 1995 and WT/ACC/RUS/17, p.32, 11 March 1997.

352   V. Drebentsov and C. Michalopoulos (1999) pp.58–9.
353   The size of the government procurement market can be indicated by one figure. In 1991, in the United States total procurement by government entities exceeded US$1 trillion, almost 20 per cent of the country's GDP. B. Hoekman and M. Kostecki (1995) p.121.
354   The following dates have been indicated for the completion of negotiations for membership: Bulgaria: 31 December 1997; Panama: 31 December 1997; Kyrgyz Republic: 31 December 1997; Latvia: 1 January 2000; Estonia: 31 December 2000.
355   WTO Document, WT/ACC/7, p.7, 10 March 1999. See also UNCTAD Document, UNCTAD/ITCD/TSB/3, p.33, 15 April 1998.
356   WTO Documents, WT/ACC/RUS/2, p.125, 2 June 1995.
357   WTO Document, WT/ACC/RUSS/4, p.190, 1 November 1995.
358   WTO Document, WT/ACC/RUS/13/Add.1, p.37, 14 October 1996.
359   M.B. Katyshev (1998) pp.4–5.
360   S.P. Boylan (1996) p.1.
361   See for example: WTO Document WT/GC/W/122, 17 December 1998; UNCTAD Document, UNCTAD/ITCD/TSB/3, p.33, 15 April 1998.
362   WTO Document, WT/ACC/RUS/4, 1 November 1995, p.177.
363   It should be noted, however, that GATT member transition economies were allowed to offer tariff bindings unrelated to base period conditions. In this aspect, they received similar treatment than developing countries which could offer 'ceiling bindings', in other words tariffs which were unrelated to past policies. They bound their tariffs at a level significantly above applied rates.
364   Annex 2 of the Agreement on Agriculture includes an illustrative list of government subsidies granted to producers that are exempt from reduction commitments. The main subsidies in this group are: general government services; research; pest and disease control; training services; extension and advisory services; inspection services; marketing and promotion services; infrastructural services; public stockholding for food security purposes, and other similar types of measure; direct payments to producers; decoupled income support; income insurance and safety-net programmes; natural disaster relief; producer and resource retirement programmes; investment aids; environmental programmes; regional assistance programmes, and other similar types of measure.
365   It is interesting to remember that in the case of Poland a hypothetical AMS was calculated for 1992, based on the share of the AMS in production values of each product category in the 1986–90 period, by applying that share to actual 1992 production values. The amount for all products was converted into US$ and is used as the base for bindings during the 1995–2000 period, where commitments are specified in US$ as well. On the other hand, Hungary has bound its domestic support and export subsidies in its inflationary domestic currency. This, and an erroneously narrow product coverage specified in the country's schedule, made the Hungarian export subsidy commitments unworkable. As a result,

Hungary asked for a waiver. WTO Documents, WT/L/238, 29 October 1997 and WT/TPR/S/40 (Trade Policy Review of Hungary), 15 June 1998.

366 Members of the Cairns Group include: Argentina, Australia, Brazil, Canada, Chile, Colombia, Fiji, Indonesia, Malaysia, Paraguay, Philippines, New Zealand, South Africa, Thailand and Uruguay. It should be mentioned that some Cairns Group countries and also the United States, even after the implementation of the Uruguay Round reduction commitments, still grant substantial domestic support to their agriculture and subsidize their exportation.

367 The description of Russian agriculture and agricultural policies is based on a major OECD Report. OECD (1998).

368 OECD (1998) p.20.

369 ECE (1999/2) p.47 and Table 2.3.7.

370 In 1997, the support given to the Russian agriculture in terms of Producer Subsidy Equivalent (PSE) was 26 per cent, the OECD average being 35 per cent in the same year. PSE figures for some other countries expressed in percentages: Czech Republic: 11; Hungary: 16; Poland: 22; EU:22; New Zealand: 3; Switzerland: 76; United States: 16. OECD (1998), Annex Table I.16.i, pp.242–5. As the PSE calculations are very sensitive to the exchange rate applied, the depreciation that followed the August 1998 crash has led to much lower PSE figures for Russia.

371 This amount 'would constitute about 18–20 per cent of total Russian GDP in 1996, Russia would not be able to support agriculture at even one fourth of this level under current economic conditions. OECD (1998) pp.72–3.

372 WTO Document, WT/ACC/4, 12 March 1996.

373 'Russia's WTO Application Advances', *International Economic Review*, January/February 1998 p.5.

374 WTO Document, WT/ACC/RUS/2, 2 June 1995 p.158.

375 WTO Document, WT/ACC/RUS/13, 23 August 1996 p.27.

376 '...the relatively advanced legislative framework it already possesses in the IPR field and many problems faced by EU rightholders in Russia, make it desirable from the Commission's point of view that Russia implement the TRIPS Agreement as a developed country Member (i.e. from the date of its accession).' EU Commission Sectoral and Trade Database, EU Commission website.

377 The basic principles of GATS include: GATS covers all services; most-favoured-nation treatment applies to all services except those which are put on the list of temporary exemptions; national treatment applies in the areas where commitments are made; transparency of regulations, which requires that laws and regulations and administrative practices are published, notified to WTO and an enquiry point is established to respond to requests for information; regulations have to be objective and reasonable; no restrictions on international payments; commitments of individual countries have to be bound; and the whole GATS system should be liberalizied through further negotiations.

378   A national schedule indicates in which service sectors, subsectors, or activities the country accords market access or national treatment. Horizontal commitments describe the measures which are applicable to all sectors. These can impose limitations across all sectors for any mode of supply. (The four modes of supply specified by the GATS include: cross-border supply; consumption of services abroad, that is the consumer moves into the territory of the supplier; commercial presence, when the supplier opens a subsidiary branch in the territory of the supplier; and presence of natural persons, that is direct physical movement of the suppliers into the territory of the consumer.) Horizontal measures may relate to conditions on market access or conditions of national treatment, or may include additional commitments. Sectoral commitments are applied to individual sectors and are grouped similarly. The term 'none' in a country schedule means that in the area specified there are no limitations or laws inconsistent with the GATS. The term 'unbound' indicates the lack of commitment which means that measures inconsistent with market access or national treatment disciplines can be maintained or introduced.

379   WTO Document, WT/ACC/7, 10 March 1999, p.98.

380   WTO Document WT/ACC/7 gives a summary of sector specific commitments and m.f.n. exemptions of Ecuador, Mongolia, Bulgaria, Panama, the Kyrgyz Republic and Latvia. Estonia's services schedule is contained in WTO Document WT/ACC/EST/28/Add.2, 7 April 1999.

381   WTO Document, WT/ACC/RUS/6, 25 October 1995, p.2. The document describes Russia's services trade regime covering both horizontal and sectoral aspects.

382   M.G. Smith (1999) p.40.

383   WTO Document, WT/ACC/RUS/9, p.76, 23 April 1996.

384   'Russian banks', *The Economist*, 22 May 1999, p.103.

385   GATT Document, L/7410, 1 March 1994, p.37.

386   In 1995, the number of these agreements reached already 300. WTO Document, WT/ACC/RUS/2, 2 June 1995, p.144.

387   'Reasonable Protection', *Expert*, No.33, 7 September 1998. In this context, the prime minister of the Kyrgyz Republic stated that the decision on the country's entry into the WTO 'is not to interfere with the interests of the states in the Customs Union'. *Press Bulletin*, Permanent Mission of the Russian Federation, Number 678 (3111), 21 January 1999.

388   *Press Bulletin*, Permanent Mission of the Russian Federation (Geneva), Number 701 (3134) 30 June 1999.

Chapter 7

389   Hungary was mentioned as a negative example, it 'lost' its native insurance market. 'If the rights of foreign insurance companies in making business in Russia are enlarged, the same fate is in store for her.' *Finansevaje Izvestija*, 22 July 1995, quoted by L. Sabelnikov (1996) p.353.

390 For a detailed analysis on the contribution of trade liberalization to economic growth, see WTO (1998) pp.32–68.
391 WTO (1998) p.47.
392 'The trade adjustment assistance scheme of the United States, for example, provides cash benefits and retraining for workers who lose their job as a result of trade. It also provides extended unemployment insurance payments, also called Trade Readjustment Allowances, relocation expenses, job search assistance and worker retraining.... A number of other countries, particularly in Western Europe, have also introduced such active labour market policies.' WTO (1998) p.47.

References

Ahdieh, R.B., *Russia's Constitutional Revolution*, (Pennsylvania: The Pennsylvania State University Press University Park, 1997).

Andreff, W., 'La réforme soviétique du commerce extérieur', *Revue francaise d'économie*, IV (1989), No.3.

Åslund, A., *How Russia Became a Market Economy*, (Washington, DC: The Brookings Institution, 1995).

Åslund, A., 'Critique of the Soviet Reform Plans', in A. Åslund (ed.) *Russia's Economic Transformation in the 1990s*, (London and Washington: Pinter, 1997).

Aven, P., 'Problems in Foreign Trade Regulation in the Russian Economic Reform', in A. Åslund (ed.), *Russia's Economic Transformation in the 1990s*, (London and Washington: Pinter, 1997).

Bergsman, J., H.G. Broadman and V. Drebentsov, 'Improving Russia's Foreign Direct Investment Policy Regime', in H.G. Broadman (ed.), *Russian Trade Policy, Reform for WTO Accession*, (Washington, DC: The World Bank, 1999).

Bestuzev-Lada, I., 'A Standard Yardstick Does Exist', *Russian Politics and Law*, 36(1998), No.6.

Blasi, J.R., M. Kroumova and D. Kruse, *Kremlin Capitalism, Privatizing the Russian Economy*, (Ithaca and London: ILR Press, an imprint of Cornell University Press, 1997).

Boone P. and B. Fedorov, 'The Ups and Downs of Russian Economic Reforms', in W.T. Woo, S. Parker and J.D. Sachs (eds), *Economies in Transition: Comparing Asia and Eastern Europe*, (Cambridge, Massachusetts and London: The MIT Press, 1998, third printing).

Boycko, M., A. Schleifer and R. Vishny, *Privatizing Russia*, (Cambridge, Massachusetts and London: The MIT Press, second printing, 1996).

Boylan, S.P., 'Organized Crime and Corruption in Russia: Implications for U.S. and International Law', *Fordham International Law Journal*, 19(1996).

van Brabant, J.M., 'The Soviet Union in the GATT? A Plea for Reform', *The International Spectator*, XXIV (1989), No.2.

Ciluffo F.J. and R. Johnstone, 'Kremlin Kapitalism', *International Economy*, XI. (1997), No.4.

Croome, J., *Reshaping the World Trading System*, (Geneva: WTO, 1995).

Domke M. and J. Hazard, 'State Trading and the Most-Favoured Nation Clause', *American Journal of International Law*, 50, (1958).

Dabrowski, M., 'The First Half-Year of Russian Transformation', in A. Åslund (ed.), *Russia's Economic Transformation in the 1990s*, (London and Washington: Pinter, 1997).

Davies, P., 'Customs Reform is Urgent in Russia', *Transition*, August 1998.

Davydov, O.D., *Inside Out, The Radical Transformation of Russian Foreign Trade, 1992–1997*, (New York: Fordham University Press, 1998).

Debrentsov V. and C. Michalopolous, 'State Trading in Russia', in H.G. Broadman (ed.), *Russian Trade Policy, Reform for WTO Accession*, (Washington, DC: The World Bank, 1999).

Economic Commission for Europe, *Economic Survey of Europe in 1991–1992*, (New York and Geneva: United Nations, 1992).

Economic Commission for Europe, *Economic Survey of Europe in 1992–1993*, (New York and Geneva: United Nations, 1993).

Economic Commission for Europe, *Economic Survey of Europe in 1993–1994*, (New York and Geneva: United Nations, 1994).

Economic Commission for Europe, *Industrial Restructuring in Selected Countries in Transition*, (New York and Geneva: United Nations, 1995).

Economic Commission for Europe, *Economic Survey for Europe in 1996–1997*, (New York and Geneva: United Nations, 1997).

Economic Commission for Europe, *Economic Survey of Europe, 1998 No.1*, (New York and Geneva: United Nations, 1998).

Economic Commission for Europe, *Economic Survey of Europe, 1998 No.3*, (New York and Geneva: United Nations, 1998).

Economic Commission for Europe, *Trends in Europe and North America*, 1998/1999, The Statistical Yearbook of the ECE, (New York and Geneva: United Nations, 1999).

Economic Commission for Europe, *Economic Survey of Europe, 1999 No.2*, (New York and Geneva: United Nations, 1999)

Elder, A., *Rubles to Dollars*, (New York, Toronto, Sydney, Tokyo and Singapore: New York Institute of Finance, 1998).

European Bank for Reconstruction and Development, *Transition Report 1997*, (London: EBRD, 1997).

European Bank for Reconstruction and Development, *Transition Report 1998*, (London: EBRD, 1998).

Frydman, R., A. Rapaczynsky and J. Turkewitz, 'Transition to a Private Property Regime in the Czech Republic and Hungary', in W.T. Woo, S. Parker and J.D. Sachs (eds), *Economies in Transition: Comparing Asia and Eastern Europe*, (Cambridge, Massachusetts and London: The MIT Press, 1998, third printing).

Gaddy C. and B.W. Ickes (1998/a), 'Underneath the Formal Economy, Why Are Russian Enterprizes Not Restructuring?', *Transition*, August 1998.

Gaddy C. and B.W. Ickes (1998/b), 'Russia's Virtual Economy', *Foreign Affairs*, 77 (1998), No.5.

Galeotti, M., 'The Mafiya and the New Russia', *Australian Journal of Politics and History*, 44 (1998), No.3.

General Agreement on Tariffs and Trade (GATT), *Basic Instruments and Selected Documents (BISD)*, (Geneva), several supplements.

GATT, Trade Policy Review, *Hungary*, Vol. I–II (Geneva, 1991).

GATT, *The Results of the Uruguay Round of Multilateral Trade Negotiations*, (Geneva: GATT Secretariat, 1994).

Goldman, M.I., *Lost Opportunity*, (New York, London: W.W. Norton & Company, 1996).

Goldman, M.I., 'The Cashless Society', *Current History*, October 1998.

Gorbachev, M., *Memoirs*, (London, New York, Toronto, Sydney, Auckland: Bantam Books, 1995).

Haus, L.A., 'The East European countries and GATT: the role of realism, mercantilism, and regime theory in explaining East–West trade negotiations', *International Organization*, 45 (1991), No.2.

Haus, L.A., *Globalizing the GATT*, (Washington, DC: The Brookings Institution, 1992).

Hellman, J.S., 'Constitutions and Economic Reform in the Post- Communist Transitions', in J.D. Sachs and K. Pistor (eds), *The Rule of Law and Economic Reform in Russia*, (Colorado and Oxford: Westview Press, 1997).

Hoekman B. and M. Kostecki, *The Political Economy of the World Trading System*, (Oxford: Oxford University Press, 1995).

Illarionov, A., R. Layard and P. Orszag, 'The Conditions of Life', in A. Åslund (ed.), *Russia's Economic Transformation in the 1990s*, (London and Washington: Pinter, 1997).

International Trade Reporter (BNA), 'Soviet Union Seeking Observer Status, May Want to Participate in New Round', No.13, 397 (26 March 1986).

International Trade Centre, *Business Guide to the Uruguay Round*, (Geneva: ITC, Commonwealth Secretariat, 1995).

Katyshev, M.B., 'Corruption in Contemporary Russia and Ways of Overcoming it', background paper for the OECD Symposium on the Rule of Law and the Development of a Market Economy in the Russian Federation, 23–24 March 1998.

Kennedy, K.C., 'The Accession of the Soviet Union to GATT', *Journal of World Trade Law*, 21 (1987), No.2.

Kostecki, M.M., *East–West Trade and the GATT System*, (London: Macmillan, 1979).

Kozul-Wright R. and P. Rayment, 'The Institutional hiatus in economies in transition and its policy consequences', *Cambridge Journal of Economics*, 21(1997), No.5.

Kramer, J.M., 'The Politics of Corruption', *Current History*, October 1998.

Landesmann, M., *Industrial Policy and the Transition in East-Central Europe*, The Vienna Institute for Comparative Economic Studies, No.196, April 1993.

Lavigne, M., 'Organized international economic co-operation after World War II', paper presented to the Symposium 'Economic reforms and the role of Asian centrally planned economies, China, Eastern Europe and the Soviet Union in global economic relations' (Helsinki, 12–16 June 1989), organized by the United Nations Department of International and Social Affairs in co-operation with World Institute for Development Economics Research.

Layard, R., Foreword to J. Sachs, *Poland's Jump to Market Economy*, (Cambridge, Massachusetts and London: The MIT Press, 1994).

Loukine, K., 'Estimation of Capital Flight from Russia: Balance of Payments Approach' *The World Economy*, 21(1998), No.5.

von Luchterhandt, Otto, 'Rechsstat Russland', *Internationale Politik*, 53(1998), No.10.

Martonyi, J., 'Eastern European countries and the GATT', in *The Political and Legal Framework of Trade Relations Between the European Community and Eastern Europe*, (ed. M. Maresceau), (Dordrecht: Kluwer Academic Publishers, 1989), pp.269–83.

Mazaev, V.D., 'Problems of Effective Performance of the Russian Legislation', OECD Symposium on the Rule of Law and the Development of a Market Economy in the Russian Federation, 23–24 March 1998.

Medvedev, S., 'Landscape After the Battle: Rethinking Democracy in Russia', *The International Spectator*, XXXII (1997), No.1.

Michalopoulos, C., (1998/a) 'WTO Accession for Countries in Transition', *Policy Research Working Paper 1934*. The World Bank, June 1998.

Michalopoulos, C., (1998/b) *The Integration of the Developing Countries into the Multilateral Trading System: Commercial Policy and Market Access*, manuscript.

Milthorp, P., 'Integration of FSU/economies in transition into the World Trade Organization', *Economics of Transition*, 5 (1997).

Naray, P., 'The End of the Foreign Trade Monopoly (The Case of Hungary)', *Journal of World Trade*, 23 (1989), No.6.

Newcity, M., 'Russian Legal Tradition and the Rule of Law', in J.D. Sachs and K. Pistor (eds) *The Rule of Law and Economic Reform in Russia*, (Colorado and Oxford: Westview Press, 1997).

Ognivtsev V. and S. Chernyshev, 'GATT: Basic Principles of Activity and Questions of the USSR's Membership', *Foreign Trade*, 11/1989, pp.29–35.

Organization for Economic Co-operation and Development, *OECD Economic Surveys, The Russian Federation*, (Paris: OECD, 1995).

Organization for Economic Co-operation and Development, *OECD Economic Surveys, The Russian Federation*, (Paris: OECD, 1997).

Organization for Economic Co-operation and Development, *Review of Agricultural Policies, Russian Federation*, (Paris: OECD, 1998).

Owen, T.C., 'Autocracy and the Rule of Law in Russian Economic History', in J.D. Sachs and K. Pistor (eds), *The Rule of Law and Economic Reform in Russia*, (Colorado and Oxford: Westview Press, 1997).

Patterson, E.L., 'Improving GATT Rules for Nonmarket Economies', *Journal of World Trade Law*, 20 (1986), No.2.

Popov, V., *A Russian Puzzle, What Makes the Russian Economic Transformation a Special Case*, (Helsinki: UNU/WIDER, 1996).

Richter, W.L., 'Soviet "Participation" in GATT: A Case for Accession', *Journal of International Law and Politics*, Vol.20(1988) No.2.

Rubin, P.H., *Promises, Promises, Contracts in Russia and other Post-Communist Economies*, (Cheltenham, UK and Northhampton, MA, USA: Edward Elgar, The Shaftbury Papers, 11, Series editor: C.K. Rowley, 1997).

Rubins, N., 'The Demise and Ressurrection of the *Propiska*: Freedom of Movement in the Russian Federation' *Harvard International Law Journal*, vol.39, No.2, Spring 1998.

Rutland P. and N. Kogan, 'The Russia Mafia: Between Hype and Reality', Transitions, 5 (1998), No.3.

Sabelnikov, L., 'Russia on the way to the World Trade Organization', *International Affairs*, 72 (1996), No.2.

Sachs, J., 'Why Russia Has Failed to Stabilize', in A. Åslund (ed.), *Russia's Economic Transformation in the 1990s*, (London and Washington: Pinter, 1997).

Sachs, J., *Poland's Jump to the Market Economy*, (Cambridge, Massachusetts and London: The MIT Press, 1994).

Savchenko L. and J. Boiarsky, 'Russian-American Roundtable on Customs Issues', *BISINIS* home page, February 1998.

Smith, M.G., 'Russia and the "General Agreement on Trade in Services" (GATS)', in H.G. Broadman (ed.), *Russian Trade Policy, Reform for WTO Accession*, (Washington, DC: The World Bank, 1999).

Tarr, D., 'Design of Tariff Policy for Russia', in H.G. Broadman (ed.), *Russian Trade Policy, Reform for WTO Accession*, (Washington, DC: The World Bank, 1999).

Vasiliev, S.A., 'Economic Reform in Russia: Social, Political, and Institutional Aspects' in A. Åslund (ed.), *Russia's Economic Transformation in the 1990s*, (London and Washington: Pinter, 1997).

Wintrobe, R., 'Privatization, the Market for Corporate Control, and Capital Flight from Russia', *The World Economy*, 21 (1998), No.5.

World Trade Organization, *Annual Report 1998*, (Geneva: World Trade Organization, 1998).

Index

DATE DUE
